PUNCH ON CHILDREN

PUNCH

ON

CHILDREN

A Panorama 1845~1865

DAVID DUFF

Designed by A.H. Eisner

FREDERICK MULLER LTD

First published in Great Britain in 1975
by Frederick Muller Ltd. London NW2 6LE

Printed and bound by A. Wheaton & Company, Exeter
ISBN: 0 584 10230 5

CONTENTS

page

Chapter 1 IN THE BEGINNING   1

2 THE CRADLE AND THE PRAM   17

3 PATERFAMILIAS   35

4 TOYS AND PASTIMES   45

5 EDUCATIONAL SUPPLEMENT   61

6 BESIDE THE SEASIDE   83

7 TRULY RURAL   105

8 LES ENFANTS TERRIBLES   119

9 THE COCKNEY KIDS   129

10 IN THE STATELY HOMES   153

11 POMPOUS PAGES   163

12 FASHION WISE   173

13 ACHES AND PAINS   187

14 LOVE   197

15 THE FIELD OF COMMERCE   209

16 THE RISING GENERATION   217

Chapter 1

IN THE BEGINNING

The lighter side of children's lives had no general news value until the 1840s. There were many sound reasons for this, the main one being that there was very little on the lighter side. Children were to be seen, and not heard. The poor raised families as an insurance policy for their old age, so that they might have a roof over their heads when they were old. The rich were interested in the continuity of their family line and estates. The poor looked upon children as an almost immediate supplement to their incomes, for there was a demand for child labour when there was none for adult. There were few entertaining stories to be told of five-year-olds who pushed trucks in tunnels three feet high, deep down in the coal mines, who scrambled all day along rambling chimneys sweeping down the soot, or who scared birds off the crops from dawn to dusk, often leaving their voices impaired for life. For them, in the eighteenth century, there was no schooling, while their more 'fortunate' brothers were sent off to endowed schools where the menus were appalling and the sadism even more so. Little fun on either count.

But a new power was on the way up. Sandwiched between the rich and the poor were the middle-classes, the shopkeepers, industrialists, professional men. Born of the Industrial Revolution, and thriving on increasing mechanical invention and the increase in commerce, those in the towns began to move away from their places of work and build for themselves comfortable houses in the suburban areas. Their way of life was comparatively secure, although they looked with fear at the discontentment and the revolutionary tendencies of the poor and at the same time bent the knee to the old time masters, the aristocracy. To this class, isolated from those above and below, came a new value — family life. A vast future lay ahead of them, and their children mattered. They made their own entertainment in their homes, but were wide open to welcome an entertainment medium. If television sets had been available in the beginning of the nineteenth century, these are the people who would have bought them. As it was, they had to bide their time for the coming of the family magazines. The visual was still way ahead.

There were newspapers, reviews, broadsheets, in plenty but they were hampered by the infamous 'taxes on knowledge'. It was a man's world, and they were aimed at men. Their contents were restricted to politics and prices, crime and vice, gossip and wars. Many of their publishers had political and religious views to back, or axes to grind. They were provocative but lacking in light entertainment.

In the 1830s, in the reign of the old and eccentric King William IV, British history began a new chapter. The Reform Bill of 1832 was the greatest organic change in the Constitution since the revolution of 1688. By extending the franchise and abolishing the 'rotten boroughs', the control of the Government was transferred from the upper to the middle classes. It also opened the door to other important political measures — such as the abolition of slavery in the British Empire in 1833, the Municipal Corporations Act of 1835 and the reduction of taxes on newspapers in the following year.

In addition, in the field of discovery and invention, new forces were altering the way of life and pointing towards the world which we know today — steamships, railways, gas lights, the electric telegraph, photography. Yet even greater than these in its impact upon family life was the accession to the Throne in 1837 of an eighteen year old girl — Victoria — and, three years later, her marriage to a handsome Prince from Germany. Babies arrived in quick succession.

Eighty years had passed since a similar situation had existed in the royal homes. In 1761 King George III had married seventeen year old Princess Charlotte of Mecklenburg-Strelitz. It was an arranged marriage, Charlotte was no beauty and the union was singularly devoid of romance. True, they had a big family, fifteen in twenty-two years as against Victoria and Albert's total of nine in seventeen years, but the brood was kept in seclusion at Kew and aroused little public interest. The boys were subjected to a spartan upbringing, and two died young. The survivors, revolting against the restrictions and discipline and endowed with abnormal sexual desires, took early to whoring. Leaving dummies in their beds and a brother to keep 'cave', they would climb out of the window and into the night. The Princesses led a convent life and, although keen to marry, were prevented from so doing by the stumbling blocks put in their path by their parents. They became known as 'the old cats of Windsor'. Three eventually achieved their goal, but not until the ages of thirty-one, forty and forty-eight respectively, and none had children who survived infancy.

With the exception of Adolphus, Duke of Cambridge, the youngest, who was a pompous bore, and talked to himself and any audience which could be persuaded to listen to him, the Princes were a profligate lot and a constant source of worry to their parents. They cluttered themselves with mistresses, morganatic wives and a tribe of bastards. Financially they were a drain on the King and the country. They collected around their names a list of nastinesses seldom, if ever, exceeded by one family — sadism, bribery, cheating, blackmail, and even, in the case of Ernest, Duke of Cumberland, incest and murder. The good in them was lost in the tidal wave of the bad. By 1816 the seven of them collectively had produced but one Heir to the Throne — George the eldest, having sired a daughter, Charlotte. This was not a product of domestic bliss, for George had at first sight taken an active dislike to the bride produced for him — Caroline of Ansbach — and showed that disapproval by spending his wedding night dead drunk in the grate. He managed one conception night, thereafter refusing to enter his wife's bed and he fought with her and his daughter for the rest of their days. Charlotte was inveigled into marriage by wily Prince Leopold of Coburg, who, by so doing, gained for himself a pension of £50,000 a year. The following year Charlotte died in childbirth. Thereafter the British public was entertained by the spectacle of middle-aged Princes chasing round Germany in search of brides of suitable family standing to beget an heir. Edward, Duke of Kent, discarded his mistress and captured a plump and voluble widow. Before dying two years later, he had sired a daughter who was named Victoria. Excepting for a few 'royal progresses' around England and Wales, organised by her mother to consolidate her position, Victoria was kept a prisoner in Kensington Palace, the victim of intrigue and the struggle for power.

This sad royal story did nothing to promote the sanctity, and happiness, of family life. Example flows from the top, and this had been drilled into young Prince Albert by his mentors before he left Coburg. There the blame for the wild ways and the immorality of the aristocracy and the upper classes, and the indiscipline and the unpleasant habits of the poor, was laid squarely on the shoulders of the young Queen's 'wicked uncles'. To him the power of the Throne, which he had in part captured, was everything, and he realised that an exemplary family life was a means of increasing it. He thus became the messiah of the middle classes who, sandwiched between wickedness and strife, were waiting for just such a creed.

Yet Albert arrived to marry Queen Victoria at a time when British home life was at its nadir. There had been a series of wet summers and the harvests of 1840 and 1841 were disastrous. Thus began 'the Hungry Forties', only to be relieved by the repeal of the Corn Laws and by Lord Shafetesbury's factory acts at the close of the decade. Starvation stalked the land, and a potato famine robbed the poor of their staple diet. The children lived on turnips, bran dumplings, cabbage stalks, pig pease, horse beans, berries and snails. A herring cut into four was a treat. If an apple core was thrown away in the street it was fought over. So desperate did the situation become that a rumour began in Luton that all children under the age of five were to be put to death by the Government.[1] The heavy tariff on foreign corn made it prohibitive and the price of foodstuffs was beyond the reach of the poor. Bread was sixpence for 2½ lbs., salt was sixpence, tea was four shillings, and sugar eightpence a lb., while wages ranged between six and ten shillings per week.

The economic plight made working conditions worse. There was wide unemployment and the enslaving of women and little children in factories aroused public indig-

[1] *Married Life of Queen Victoria.* Jerrold, p. 149

nation and a hatred of the better off. An old man in Huddersfield recalled his youth:

> Poor mother died when I was between two and three. My eldest sister went to work in the factory very early. I soon had to follow ... What with hunger and hard usage I bitterly got it burned into me — I believe it will stay while life shall last. We had to be up at 5 in the morning to get to the factory, ready to begin work at 6, then work while 8, when we stopped ½ an hour for breakfast, then work to 12 noon; for dinner we had 1 hour, then work while 4. We then had ¼ an hour for tea, and tea if anything was left, then commenced work again on to 8.30. If any time during the day had been lost, we had to work while 9 o'clock, and so on every night till it was all made up. Then we went to what was called home. Many times I have been asleep when I had taken my last spoonful of porridge — not even washed, we were so overworked and underfed. I used to curse the road we walked on. I was so weakly and feeble I used to think it was the road would not let me go along with the others.

> We had not always the kindest of masters. I remember the master's trap, 5 or 6 feet long, about ½ in. broad and ½ in. thick. He kept it on the ginney at his right hand, so we could not see when he took hould of it. But we could not mistake its lessons; for he got hould of it nearly in the middle, and it would be a rare thing if we did not get 2 cuts at one stroke. I have reason to believe on one occasion he was somewhat moved to compassion, for the end of his strap striped the skin of my neck about 3 in. long. When he saw the blood and cut, he actually stopped the machine, came and tied a handkerchief round my neck to cover it up. I have been felled to the floor many times by the ruler on the top of the carding, about 8 or 9 feet long, iron hoop at each end. This was done as a change from the strap .... Soon afterwards, that Heaven-sent Messenger, Lord Shaftesbury, got a bill passed to shorten the hours in the factory. I read of his Lordship houlding a meeting in Leeds, where some 200 children or more were at the meeting, and not one of them but was a cripple, as also were my sister and myself crippled for life ....[1]

As a natural result such a state of affairs directed criticism towards the way of life at Buckingham Palace and Windsor and many suggestions were made as to how economies might be effected there. One was that the gold lace should be stripped from the liveries of the royal servants and sold for the benefit of the poor. This did not amuse Prince Albert at all, as such impertinences were neither encouraged nor tolerated in the land from which he came.

The Queen made little gestures to show her concern, but as yet she was inexperienced and gained small reward. She declared a national day of fasting, a sacrifice which meant little out of the ordinary for the starving poor but for the royal household ended in a mammoth hot supper as the clock struck midnight. She organised a stupendous charity ball, a *Bal Masque,* the avowed intent of which was to stimulate

[1] *The Hungry Forties: Life under the Bread Tax.*

British trade. She appeared, jewel-laden, as Queen Philippa, escorted by Albert posing as Edward III. Many of the guests hired suits of armour and the revelries, lit by over five hundred gas jets, went on until the workers in the mean streets struggled up into another day. On the following Sunday a preacher boomed out from his pupit: "When Charity takes to dancing, it ceases to be Charity and becomes a wanton."[1] Fortunately, in latter years under the democratic influence of John Brown, the Queen learned more practical ways of relief and would carry round with her a bag of assorted coins which she would hand out to the needy. A blind beggar singing 'Abide with me' on Windsor bridge was much surprised and delighted when the royal carriage stopped and he was handed half a crown.

As Victoria and Albert 'nested' and fitted out their nurseries, there was another birth in London. It was of a magazine. Its name was *Punch,* and it arrived in the same year as the birth of the Heir to the Throne — 1841. It was to make a deep and strong

THE NEW PAGE HONESTLY ACCOUNTS FOR HIS HONESTY.

"*I am glad to perceive, Dixy, that you are a good boy, and do not make free with the Almonds and Raisins.*"

"*Halmonds and Raisings, Mum? No, Mum, not if I knows it! Why they caught me once, Mum, they did! They'd Counted 'em, they'ad!*"

contribution to the value of family life. It was to enrich the long hours, in the lamplight by the fire's moving picture. It was to amuse, to titivate, to educate, to bind parents and children in a common interest, to right wrongs, to warn, and to introduce the visual into the field of entertainment. It was a household treasure in the forties and, little changing, was by the chairside as children grew to be grandparents and the cycle began once again.

Punch dominated the field of caricature from its inception and for a quarter of a century was alone in its glory. It is this quarter of a century which this book covers, until the magic number of '50' was embossed in gold on the dark green covers of the biannual bound editions. Twenty-five years of the weeks from January to June, and from July to December. And what a period of change it was. At its beginning newly-wed Victoria and Albert were travelling around England in a coach. At its end the Black Widow of Windsor was moving the length and breadth of Britain, and much of Europe, in her luxurious special trains. In 1841 no reigning monarch had visited Scotland since the days of Charles I, with the exception of George IV who, braving the bloody ghost of the Duke of Cumberland, the 'Butcher' of Culloden, had spent a short time in Edinburgh in 1822. By 1865 there was a fine and established royal home on Deeside and the British Queen was an integral part of the Balmoral landscape, happier there than when at Buckingham Palace or Windsor. The Chartist movement had petered out. The Crimean War had jolted Britain from the military stagnation that was the legacy of Waterloo. The Great International Exhibitions had set the stage for a new industrial revolution.

In France the reign of King Louis Philippe had ended with his flight to Newhaven under the alias of Mr. Smith; Napoleon III had travelled from London to Paris to take up the reins of power, but by 1865 the evening sun was setting in on the spectacular day of the Second Empire. In Germany Bismarck had risen out of the ashes of weak King Frederick William IV, the Schleswig-Holstein war had been fought and won and, with Austria and France next for the chopping block, the German Empire was in embryo. In America, North and South had been at one another's throats, four million men involved in four years of strife. The end result was the preservation of the Union, the abolition of slavery and a host of social and political changes.

This quarter of a century saw the passing of many great men, Lord Melbourne, Sir Robert Peel, the Duke of Wellington, Prince Albert the Consort, King Leopold of the Belgians and Lord Palmerston. By 1865 the girl-Queen of 1841 was a grandmother seven times over. Three of her children were married — the Princess Royal to the Crown Prince of Prussia, Princess Alice to Louis, heir to the Grand Duchy of Hesse and by the Rhine, and Albert Edward, Prince of Wales, to Princess Alexandra of Denmark.

It was an age when Britain, Europe and America changed gear and speeded up, when the balance of power was altered, when the Dominions were in the making, when explorers ventured into the secret places of the world, when electricity and photography were weaned, when communications lessened distance and great ships conquered the oceans, when medical science brought relief and hope. It was an age under the influence of Prince Albert and Palmerston, and it gave place to the gay days of Albert Edward, Prince of Wales, and Disraeli; the days of the new rich and the international set, who sparkled and sinned on the merry-go-rounds of Marlborough House and Sandringham.

Punch — what a name! Punch and Judy, and Toby the dog, bringing back a flood of memories of the seaside and parties, outings and fairgrounds, to a century of children. Abbreviated from Punchinello, the origins of the famous puppet are a part of Italian mythology. There he is *Pulcinella* or *Policinella.* Some say the original was a grape-gatherer of Acerra near Naples, whose name was Puccio d'Aniello. When some strolling players came to the village Puccio joined in their act and outshone them all. They asked him to join their troupe and he became their star. When Puccio died, the troupe kept his memory alive by dressing up one of their members in his clothes. He wore a mask and imitated Puccio's voice and movements.

Another theory has it that Punch stems from *pulcina,* Italian for a chicken. Chicken was a word of endearment for a child, and thus it became to mean a little child or a puppet. Certainly Punch's nose resembles a beak and the nasal squeak is not far removed from the chatter of the young inmates of the hen-house. At any rate by the mid-seventeenth century *Pulcinella* had become a caricature of a country clown, with hooked nose and shrill voice, boastful, up to all kinds of tricks but capable of shrewd remarks.

In the reign of Louis XIV the puppet reached France, where it was called *Polichinelle.* There were traces of him in England in Stuart days, but it was not until the arrival of King William of Orange that he became established. The Dutch were experts on puppet mechanism and made the show more lifelike and intricate. Soon he was appearing at Covent Garden. In those days 'Judy' was sometimes known as 'Joan' and a cat replaced the dog.

There was also much mystery, and many claimants, concerning the paternity of *Punch,* the magazine. M.H. Spielman, author of *The History of Punch,* published in 1895, was of the opinion that Henry Mayhew and Ebenezer Landells were the real founders:

> "Yet although it was not .... Henry Mayhew who was the actual initiator of *Punch,* it was unquestionably he to whom the whole credit belongs of having developed Landell's specific idea of a 'Charivari', and of its conception in the form it took. Though not the absolute author of its existence, he was certainly the author of its literary and artistic being, and to that degree, as he was wont to claim, he was its *founder.*"

After a number of discussions between the original staff of the planned, and as yet unnamed, magazine, a prospectus was drawn up by Mark Lemon. It was written on three pages, of which the first can be seen on the following page.

It can be seen that the main title was crossed out by Lemon before he had completed it. It reads — 'The Fun ———.' It is believed that, if he had completed it, it would have read 'The Funny Dogs' or 'The Funny Dogs with Comic Tales.' Now the settling of the name was the all important point, and Spielman tells how it was done:

> Hodder declares that it was Mayhew's sudden inspiration. Last asserted that when "somebody" at the *Edinburgh Castle* meeting spoke of the paper, like a good mixture of punch being nothing without the Lemon, Mayhew

caught at the idea and cried, "A capital idea: We'll call it *Punch:*"

There were other amendments to Lemon's prospectus. Financial reasons caused an increase in the price from twopence to threepence and the date of publication was delayed. In the event the first number of *Punch* came out on 17th July 1841, at 13, Wellington Street, Strand, London. It had been preceded by an advertising campaign and the demand was brisk, two editions of five thousand copies each being sold in two days.

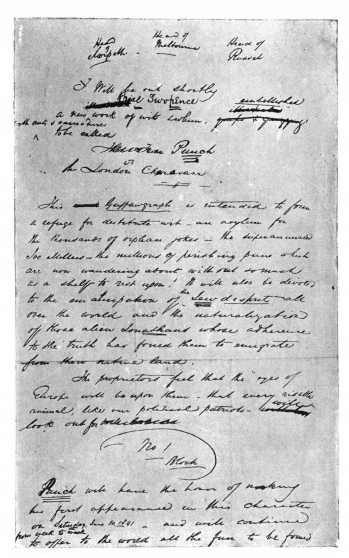

The first page of the original prospectus of "PUNCH,"
in the handwriting of Mark Lemon. 1841.

8

The first numbers of *Punch* were satirical, biting and political, reflecting the spirit of the 'broadsheets' and the agony of 'the Hungry Forties'. Little space yet for children's fun. Soon the names of the artists became household words, and their work eagerly awaited — William Newman, A.S. Henning, John Leech (with his sign-manual of a leech in a bottle), William Makepeace Thackeray (with his big 'T'), Richard Doyle. In those early days there was no process which allowed drawings to be increased or decreased in scale. The wood-block had to be of the same size as the artist's original. In addition, when there were moments of crisis (and no magazine exists without a plethora of those) there was pressure on the time allowed for the wood-engraving and thus there is a lack of good finish to many of the early pictures.

Queen Victoria first featured on *Punch's* pages in September 1841. On 30th August she had an interview with her new Prime Minister, Sir Robert Peel.

It was a moment which she had both dreaded and feared. She was heart-broken at losing her friend and adviser, Lord Melbourne, whose Government had fallen. She disliked the cold, aloofness of Peel, with whom she had had already, one bitter row.

THE LETTER OF INTRODUCTION.

The artist gets the look in her eyes correctly, but otherwise is somewhat wide of the mark. Peel was certainly not so smilingly confident when he came into the Presence. The dog (which is not recognisable as one of the Palace troop) appears to be but waiting his mistress's word to rip the Premier's trousers. The major error is the Queen's twenty-four inch waist—she was seven months pregnant.

THE FIRST TOOTH.

The Prince of Wales, born in November of that year, did not receive visual recognition until 1843, an indication of the almost complete lack of news value of infants. He is, as his mother points out, cutting his first tooth. To distract his attention from the crisis, the doctor blows a toy trumpet and offers soldiers, while Lady Lyttelton competes from the floor with a plaything made of coral.

Next year young Albert Edward appeared again, this time catching the gold fish in Mamma's bowl. It was an indication that the everyday pranks of children were

ROYAL SPORT.

It will be in the recollection of our readers that a handsome rod (which turns out to be really a fishing-rod after all), was a little while ago presented to the Prince of WALES. His Royal Highness has lately had some capital sport with this rod, having succeeded in capturing several of his Mamma's gold fish, one of which was as big as a dace and weighed six ounces. It was very nearly pulling the Prince in.

beginning to have an appeal.

There were few pictures of the other royal children, but there was soon plenty of material, both in text and picture, about Prince Albert. *Punch* was very critical, and very rude, about the Queen's husband from Germany. It considered, and rightly so, that he was a very expensive appendage and too fond of money. It deplored his shooting tastes, in particular his participation in the mass murder of deer penned into enclosures from which they had no chance of escape. It suspected, and again rightly, that he was exerting undue influence in the field of politics. Although the Prince received some rough handling during the planning period for the Great International Exhibition, he gained some bouquets when the Hyde Park fiesta proved a resounding success. He was later suspected of intrigue and bias at the time of the Crimean war, but thereafter, for his last few tired years, he was left in peace. On 21st December 1861 *Punch* laid a noble wreath upon his memory:

> *It* was too soon to die.
> Yet, might we count his years by triumphs won,
> By wise, and bold, and Christian duties done,
> It were no brief eventless history.

What contrast was this with the drawing which had appeared fifteen years earlier of the Prince, his wife and five young children standing before Buckingham Palace. A request had been made that public money should be spent on improving the accommodation in the royal home; Albert had complained that his children were quartered in attic rooms intended for servants, that all day long they were subjected to the noise of hammering coming from the Palace workshop below, and that the smell of oil and glue was stifling. The Lords of the Treasury eventually allowed an estimate of £150,000.

Punch was incensed and thus pictured the Prince making his appeal for relief, his audience — barefooted street arabs, dressed in rags.

A CASE OF REAL DISTRESS.

"Good People, pray take compassion upon us. It is now nearly seven years since we have either of us known the blessing of a Comfortable Residence. If you do not believe us, good people, come and see where we live, at Buckingham Palace, and you will be satisfied that there is no deception in our story. Such is our Distress, that we should be truly grateful for the blessing of a comfortable two-pair back, with commonly decent Sleeping Rooms for our Children and Domestics. With our slender means, and an Increasing Family, we declare to you that we do not know what to do. The sum of One Hundred and Fifty Thousand Pounds will be all that will be required to make the needful alterations in our dwelling. Do, good people, bestow your Charity to this little amount, and may you never live to feel the want of so small a trifle."

By 1845 *Punch* was growing up. Although not yet free of the newspaper taxes, it was clearly catering for a wider audience, an audience whose taste was more for the social and domestic. More space was being given to the sayings and doings of the young, and it is from this time until 1865 that the main body of these drawings is taken.

This volume is in no way intended to be a review of early Victorian childhood. Children are timeless, and many of the jokes could well fit into the 1970s. It is a collection of the wit and the fun of the young. Although *Punch* was ever quick to attempt to right the wrong — as the picture below, which puts the lot of the London street arab into balance, shows — the main target was the talent to amuse.

TELESCOPIC PHILANTHROPY.

LITTLE LONDON ARAB. "PLEASE 'M, AIN'T WE BLACK ENOUGH TO BE CARED FOR?"

(*With* MR. PUNCH's *Compliments to* LORD STANLEY.)

In chronicling the past there is often a tendency amongst writers to stress the conditions at the top and at the bottom, at their best and at their worst, the times of crisis and drama. Yet, in all ages, there are 'ordinary people' and 'ordinary days', and it needs but a balanced perspective of the conditions of those times to bring everyday life into focus. There were many practices, customs and cruelties in the nineteenth century which appal us in the twentieth, but then in the 1840s, people thought much the same about goings-on in the eighteenth century, for instance the impaling of the heads of Scotsmen on poles after the rising of '45.

In assessing the drawings it must be remembered that *Punch's* subsidiary title, from its inception, was *'the London Charivari'*. It was the satirical journal of the capital. Transport and the mass media of today have brought a degree of sameness in custom, language, thought and way of life to places as far apart as Salford and Sunderland, Plymouth and Aberdeen, but a century and a quarter ago the hedges that encircled differing areas were very thick. A joke which tickled the palate of the Londoner might leave but a look of blank non-comprehension or even disapproval on the face of the Yorkshireman or the Welshman. *Punch* carried a drawing of two inhabitants in a village in the North-East studying a passerby in the street. One asks the other who the man was. On being told that he was a stranger, the first replies: 'Heave half a brick at him.' In those days strangers began at the parish boundary.

Perspective can best be obtained by taking a journey back through time to the week when the drawing was published. Then we have but two considerations to weigh-up — the thoughts in the mind of the artist and the decisions taken at the editorial conference round the famous 'table' where the contents of *Punch* have always been decided. Let us leave home or lodgings with the artist, in, perhaps, St. John's Wood or Westminster. Let us look into his mind. His thoughts are concerned with immediate sights and problems, and from them comes inspiration. If he takes a cab, the repartee of the driver, or of an urchin who opens the door for him, may provide material for a drawing. If he travels by a horse bus, the conductor's comments are a rich source of possibilities. The boy who sweeps the street crossing is full of quick wit. The chimney sweep's boy, black with soot, excites a wave of indignation. There is a sardonic smile for the dignified old lady who is followed by a fat page leading her little dog. The butcher's boys are shouting insults at one another. Our artist calls in at the apothecary's and finds a child of ten in charge while the master attends to other business. In the park he sees the nannies pushing their charges in wooden-wheeled prams and the young swells showing off on their ponies.

After a morning's work our artist might have lunch with his contemporaries. What would they talk about? Strangely enough, much the same as men in London in similar circumstances talk about today— the Channel tunnel, the possibility of the introduction of the metric system, the nonsense of the new postal codes — surely the postman can find Knightsbridge? Share prices, would be discussed, of course, particularly those of railways and the traffic jams, which were becoming unbearable as the streets were dug up for the laying of gas and water mains. What was the solution? The concensus of opinion was against tunnelling and underground trains. Why could they not have overhead buses drawn by endless cables? Holidays were fast becoming a major topic of conversation — for the single Boulogne, or perhaps, rather ambitiously, the Rhine, and there were jokes about venturing to Scotland, if one could shoot, and if one had a kilt. For the married there was always Ramsgate again, as usual — the sand, the donkeys, so nice for the children, but there were endless tales about mean landladies. Like children, artists and authors and journalists change very little.

Open the pages of *Punch* anywhere throughout its long history and one finds an emphasis on current trends. These are not only of public interest, but also very much in the artist's mind. Examples from the 1920s were 'Oxford bags', 'the shingle', and 'the Black Bottom'. Fashion has always been foremost among the trends and in the period with which we deal the crinoline and those hats with very wide brims were the targets, both giving plenty of scope for introducing childish pranks. Then there was the photograph, and in particular the 'carte-de-visite' which one left behind when 'calling'. *Punch* had no mercy for the ageing spinster who considered that the dew was still upon her, or for the mother who harboured false ideas about the beauty of her children. The same applied to the invasion of Italian organ grinders, who were decidedly unpopular.

Some current happenings were stressed because they effected the artists' comfort and peace of mind. Garrotting, for example. In the winter of 1862-3 this particularly nasty form of robbery with violence became common in London's streets and in the natural course was uppermost in the mind on the journey home on dark evenings. Every dark corner might hide a 'garrotter', every footstep behind was deeply suspect. The methods put forward for counteracting the menace were many and inventive, ranging from a neck collar with spikes on it to a metal cage enclosing the body.

Then there was the 'Volunteer Movement'. In 1859 the warlike attitude of France under Emperor Napoleon III aroused military enthusiasm throughout Britain and, to meet the threat of invasion, a volunteer force was called into existence by royal command. To *Punch's* artists it was regarded as the nineteenth century equivalent of 'Dad's Army'. If they did not join themselves, they all had friends who did, and these appear to have been short and round and very unfit. The children had the greatest fun imitating them as they made their way to parades. Queen Victoria, on the other hand, took the movement very seriously, reviewing twenty thousand volunteers in Hyde Park in June 1860. Whenever possible she would attend their military exercises. When she was watching them one scorching hot summer's day, a company, perspiring and puffing, passed her by at the double. She turned to Lord Palmerston, who was accompanying her, and remarked: "Don't you think that there is rather a ———." She put her handkerchief to her nose. "That," replied the Prime Minister, "is what we call *esprit de corps.*"

Sometimes there are jokes in *Punch* for which it is difficult to find a point, in most cases the answer lies in some topical happening now lost in time, but certain drawings were not understood even by contemporary readers, a classic example can be found on page 16.

It appeared on 6th February 1847. It was drawn by Thackeray, and Mark Lemon was then the editor, and as both were men of brilliant wit, it is safe to assume that there was a point somewhere. Yet no one could see it. One thwarted lover of humour offered 'a reward of £500 and a free pardon' to anyone who could furnish the explanation — But the mystery remained unsolved.

HORRID TRAGEDY IN PRIVATE LIFE!

Chapter 2

THE CRADLE AND THE PRAM

Punch made little mention of pregnancy and child-birth. There was no place for it in a magazine devoted to satire and comedy and open to reading by all the family. There was, however, one drawing on the subject, both macabre and funny. At two in the morning 'Papa' is told by the midwife that the doctor must be called. It was in the time when garrotters waited for their prey in the dark streets and 'Papa' is in some trepidation about the trip. So he picks up the cradle which is waiting for the new baby and places it over his head, thus protecting his neck from attack from the rear.

Infant mortality was one hundred and fifty per thousand births in the 1850s and varied little until the end of the century. Then, with increasing medical knowledge and welfare services, the figure fell dramatically and by 1927 was down to sixty nine.

The high birth and death rate of infants was responsible for a lesser degree of importance, of joy and sadness, being attached to the occasions than applies today. Mrs. Peel studied the reactions of both the rich and the poor.[1]

In the diary of a lady of fashion of the 1840s, there are but casual references to her confinements. She begins one page with 'Baby born', and fills in the rest with detailed information regarding domestic matters such as staff troubles and jam making. A few weeks later comes the entry — 'Woke this morning to find that my Treasure

[1] *A Hundred Wonderful Years.*

17

had passed away'. There is no further reference to the death of her son, and he was the only boy in her family of six. The general idea was that God sent the children, and it was up to Him if He wanted to take them away.

No one worried about smelly drains — they were rather a joke and had their uses. When they smelled really badly, it was a warning that rain was imminent. Queen Victoria's loo at Buckingham Palace spilled out onto a flat roof. It was not until after she lost her husband from typhoid in 1861, and ten years later very, very nearly lost her eldest son through the same cause, that she became more circumspect and an expert on water closets. When visiting Germany, she ordered, in advance, that one should be constructed, to suit her particular size.

Bad sanitation decimated the poor. Many babies never got a chance, but those who survived to become adults were often hardened to infection and could even drink water from ponds covered in green scum. However, there was another side to the high mortality rate, for if death had not thinned down the families they would have found it even harder to make ends meet. As one old lady put it:

> "No, I didn't seem to hold with marryin' — saw too much of it. Saw me own sisters. There wasn't Parish nurses when I was young, nor chloroform. If the women died, they died. People took things as they come in those days, and if it hadn't been for some of the children dyin', how'd the poor ever have brought up a family?"

And thus another:

> "Born in 1829 I was, and eldest of ten. People had fam'lies as were fam'lies then and took what the Almighty sent them. Seven on us died, and I being the eldest can call to mind that I wasn't sorry, though Mother, who was a soft-hearted woman, 'ud cry a bit .... Fayther were a hard man an' took strap to us if we didn't behave. He'd take t'strape to Mother too ....My gran-niece lives over at L——— and thinks herself put to it with three children. Feeds them on salmon and pickles —— hee-hee —— she in silk stockings and a silk blouse and not content then. I'd like to see 'er husband take the strap to *'er,* I would."

And a third:

> "Twenty I was when I married, and I'd been to service since I were ten years old ... Up to a fortnight before my second boy came I worked, and then I was obliged to give up. I'd had to spend a bit on getting things ready, and I prayed God the baby would come quick so as I could get to work again, for my husband had been out for months owing to his arm, and folk not wanting a man as couldn't work like others. Every day I prayed God that the baby'd be born, but it didn't come for three weeks and then we'd but a few pence left. I was up and about a week after. Miserable I did feel. I sat there and cried, I did, with longing for a cup o'tea."

Now, however, there came to mothers, at least the privileged ones, a longing more potent than that for a cup of tea. It was for chloroform. In 1847 Sir James Simpson was the first to apply anasthesia by ether to midwifery practice. '*Etherial* confinements,' Fanny Kemble called them, and quoted a friend who "expresses some anxiety touching the authority of the Book of Genesis, which she thinks may be impaired if women continue, by means of ether, to escape from the special curse pronounced against them for their share in the original sin."[1] She was firm too in her condemnation of society ladies who gave parties where whiffs of chloroform took the place of the customary alcoholic beverage.

It was Dr. John Snow of Edinburgh who, after considerable success with ether, turned his attention to chloroform and his moment of triumph came when he was summoned to attend at the birth of the Queen's eighth child in 1853. Only an ounce of chloroform, administered from a rolled up handkerchief, was used, but the patient declared that "the effect was soothing, quieting and delightful beyond measure". She may well have ignored the Book of Genesis in her belief that any association with Albert could not possibly come under the heading of sin.

Forward-looking as Victoria was as regards the relief of natal pain, she was in retard when it came to breast feeding. She regarded women who undertook this natural function as 'cows' and so expressed herself to her daughters. She believed that certain inherited weaknesses could be eliminated through the milk of a wet nurse. Albert had expressed the opinion that the royal family was apt to be lymphatic and that a dose of the fire lurking behind brown eyes would be a good thing. For that eighth child, Leopold, she hired a woman from the Highlands who arrived in a cap and a plaid shawl and spoke no English. The experiment was not a success, although no blame can be laid on Scotland's breast as Leopold was an haemophiliac. When Princess Alice's first child was born at Windsor in 1863, the Queen chose as the wet nurse a pretty Irish girl, who had to be bathed before she could go into service. On this occasion the result was a definite plus, as the baby girl, thus tended, became the mother of Earl Mountbatten of Burma

Queen Victoria's aversion to breast feeding was strange as she herself had been fed by her mother. Her father regarded 'maternal nutriment' as a most interesting and novel experiment, and observed the process closely.

Children were not introduced into the pages of *Punch* until they had passed the age which the Queen referred to as the 'frog' stage. Occasional drawings featuring babies began to appear in the 1850s, but often with a sly dig at the new trend for the open display of motherly love, as if to say that the British matron had deteriorated since Waterloo. The feeling was in line with that adopted towards lap dogs, spinster ladies with 'Fido' on a lead being a favourite target. The message was easy to read — dogs were meant for hunting and fighting, keeping guard and working on the farm.

Prams made good pictures — hoodless, single or double seaters with three wheels of wood, they were little comfort for bouncing babies and hard to push on the rough roads. Along with the pram went the nurse.

Nanny was an essential element in domestic life, from the middle classes up to Blenheim Palace. At the lower end of the scale they worked alone; at the top, if family size demanded, there might be as many as four, 'head', 'under', 'night' and 'maid'. In the main a wonderful breed, their flag came down with the sunset of the British Empire.

[1] *Records of Later Life* ·

A good nurse built good character into her charges, just as a good head groom schooled them into fine horsemen. If a family, which could afford to employ a first-rate nanny employed one who was not, the fault lay with the mother, often too engaged in her social life to check references and to oversee. 'Rogues' sometimes penetrated into high places. One entered York Cottage, Sandringham, in 1895. Her charge was Prince David of York afterwards Edward VIII and Duke of Windsor. Before carrying him into the drawing-room for the evening session with the Duke and Duchess of York, this nanny would indulge in an energetic session of pinching and arm twisting. As could only be expected, on entering the parental presence young David sobbed and bawled. Neither sailor George, nor Mary his wife, were experts on, or enthusiastic about small babies and, proud as they were of their achievement, they found the noise emanating from him both annoying and irritating. It was some time before the Duchess discovered that the perverse nurse was attempting to prove that she had more power over the King-to-be than had his parents.

The root cause of such idiosyncrasies was usually to be found in the lack of natural sex and in the transference of the maternal instinct to another's child. In the bastion of the nursery sexual indulgence was both impossible and unthinkable, and the social code of the staff in a big house was stern and clear cut. Girls entered their apprenticeship early and were kept under an eagle eye. By the time they reached the status of nanny in charge, they were no longer young. Working for the most part, away from their home area, they had no local social contact, and their afternoons off were spent visiting other nannies in other nurseries.

Sex was subjugated to duty and to the whole way of life. Girls coming from poor homes became accustomed to the comfort and security of the big house — regular meals, big rooms and good fires, parks and gardens, holidays and travelling. To most, sex on a hard bed in a cottage and a husband with but a few shillings a week seemed poor exchange. There was a remote chance that a nanny might keep the best of both worlds by marrying the coachman or the head gardener — butlers seldom indulged — but most stayed on in their posts through two generations, or even three, becoming the corner-stone and mentor of a vast family. They were renowned for their longevity and ended their days in a quiet room in the west wing. That, however, came later, the nannies, as we know and recall them, were all young in the 1850s and *Punch* appears to have regarded them as suitable consorts for army sergeants.

There was little regarding infancy in the written columns of the magazine, but there was one adventure of babyhood which was considered to be of sufficient interest to occupy a page of verse. It was taken from a news item in *The Times* of 14th February 1850:—

The Lamentable Ballad
OF
THE FOUNDLING OF SHOREDITCH.

From the Times of Feb. 14.

OME all ye Christian people, and listen to my tail,
It is all about a doctor was travelling by the rail,
By the Heastern Counties Railway (vich the shares I don't desire),
From Ixworth town in Suffolk, vich his name did not transpire.

A travelling from Bury this Doctor was employed
With a gentleman, a friend of his, vich his name was CAPTAIN LOYD;
And on reaching Marks Tey Station, that is next beyond Colchest--er, a lady entered into them most elegantly dressed.

She entered into the Carriage all with a tottering step,
And a pooty little Bayby upon her bussum slep;
The gentlemen received her with kindness and siwillaty,]
Pitying this lady for her illness and debillaty.

She had a fust class ticket, this lovely lady said,
Because it was so lonesome she took a secknd instead.
Better to travel by secknd class, than sit alone in the fust,
And the pooty little Baby upon her breast she nust.

A seein of her cryin, and shiverin and pail,
To her spoke this surging, the Ero of my tail;
Saysee you look unwell, Ma'am, I'll elp you if I can,
And you may tell your case to me, for I'm a meddicle man.

"Thank you, Sir," the lady said, "I ony look so pale,
Because I ain't accustom'd to travelling on the Rale;
I shall be better presnly, when I've ad some rest:"
And that pooty little Baby she squeeged it to her breast.

So in conwersation the journey they beguiled,
CAPTING LOYD and the medical man, and the lady and the child,
Till the warious stations along the line was passed,
For even the Heastern Counties' trains must come in at last.

When at Shoreditch tumminus at lenth stopped the train,
This kind meddicle gentleman proposed his aid again.
"Thank you, Sir," the lady said, "for your kyindness dear;
My carridge and my osses is probbibly come here.

Will you old this baby, please, vilst I step and see?"
The Doctor was a famly man: "That I will," says he.
Then the little child she kist, kist it very gently,
Vich was sucking his little fist, sleeping innocently.

With a sigh from her art, as though she would have bust it,
Then she gave the doctor the child—wery kind he nust it:
Hup then the lady jumped hoff the bench she sate from,
Tumbled down the carridge steps and ran along the platform.

Vile hall the other passengers vent upon their vays,
The Capting and the Doctor sate there in a maze;
Some vent in a Homminibus, some vent in a Cabby,
The Capting and the Doctor vaited vith the babby.

There they sate looking queer, for an hour or more,
But their feller passinger neather on 'em sore:
Never, never, back again did that lady come
To that pooty sleeping Hinfnt a suckin of his Thum!

What could this pore Doctor do, bein treated thus,
When the darling Baby woke, cryin for its nuss?
Off he drove to a female friend, vich she was both kind and mild,
And igsplained to her the circumstance of this year little child.

That kind lady took the child instantly in her lap,
And made it very comforable by giving it some pap;
And when she took its close off, what d' you think she found?
A couple of ten pun notes sewn up, in its little gownd!

Also in its little close, was a note which did conwey,
That this little baby's parents lived in a handsome way:
And for its Headucation they reglarly would pay,
And sirtingly like gentlefolks would claim the child one day,
If the Christian people who'd charge of it would say,
Per adwertisement in the *Times*, where the baby lay.

Pity of this bayby many people took,
It had such pooty ways and such a pooty look;
And there came a lady forrard (I wish that I could see
Any kind lady as would do as much for me;

And I wish with all my art, some night in *my* night gownd,
I could find a note stitched for ten or twenty pound)—
There came a lady forrard, that most honorable did say,
She'd adopt this little baby, which her parents cast away.

While the Doctor pondered on this hoffer fair,
Comes a letter from Devonshire, from a party there,
Hordering the Doctor, at its Mar's desire,
To send the little Infant back to Devonshire.

Lost in apoplexity, this pore meddicle man,
Like a sensable gentleman, to the Justice ran;
Which his name was MR. HAMMILL, a honorable beak,
That takes his seat in Worship Street four times a week.

"O Justice!" says the Doctor, "instrugt me what to do,
I've come up from the country, to throw myself on you;
My patients have no doctor to tend them in their ills,
(There they are in Suffolk without their draffts and pills!)

"I've come up from the country, to know how I'll dispose
Of this pore little baby, and the twenty pun note, and the clothes,
And I want to go back to Suffolk, dear Justice, if you please,
And my patients wants their Doctor, and their Doctor wants his feez."

Up spoke MR. HAMMILL, sittin at his desk,
"This year application does me much perplesk;
What I do advise you, is to leave this babby
In the Parish where it was left, by its mother shabby."

The Doctor from his Worship sadly did depart—
He might have left the baby, but he hadn't got the heart,
To go for to leave that Hinnocent, has the laws allows,
To the tender mussies of the Union House.

Mother, who left this little one on a stranger's knee,
Think how cruel you have been, and how good was he!
Think, if you've been guilty, innocent was she;
And do not take unkindly this little word of me:
Heaven be merciful to us all, sinners as we be!

HAPPY AND HUME-OROUS.

IT is not often that MR. HUME indulges in a joke—for he is economical even of his wit—and he avoids humorous as well as all other extravagance. He did, however, a few evenings ago indulge in a sally, which, though coming from the venerable JOSEPH, might have been mistaken for an "Old JOE," but which was really of a rather fresh and buoyant character. He rose for the purpose of moving for an address to HER MAJESTY, recommending the abolition of the Lord Lieutenant of Ireland, and at the same time gave notice of a motion proposing a drawback on bricks—the point evidently bing the coupling of the Lord Lieutenant with bricks in general. Now the antecedents of the present Lord Lieutenant prove him to be a brick in the largest sense of the word, and hence arises the combination to which we have thought ourselves justified in prefixing the epithets "happy and Hume-orous."

TO BE DISPOSED OF.—A small Joke Business, doing from six to seven Puns per day. The dinner connection is good, and capable of improvement, with an average stock of linen, and appetite moderate. No professed punster or pickpocket need apply. The concern is only parted with in consequence of the proprietor going into another line—the penny-a-line. Any person retiring from the latter business, and having on hand a few Sea Serpents, early Gooseberries, Mermaids, or Earthquakes, not much the worse for wear, may hear of a purchaser.

A FACT FROM THE NURSERY.

Nurse. "MY GOODNESS GRACIOUS, MISS CHARLOTTE, YOU MUSN'T PLAY WITH THOSE SCISSORS!"

Miss Charlotte. "I'M NOT PLAYING WITH 'EM, NURSE DEAR—I'M CUTTING 'ITTLE BRUDDER'S NAILS!"

A FACT.—NOTICE WITH A VENGEANCE.

Fond, but Stout Parent. "YES, SHE DOES TAKE NOTICE, SO; AND SHE'S BEGINNING TO KNOW ALL THE BEASTS IN THE ARK BY NAME, TOO. THERE, BABY, WHAT'S THIS?" (*Holding up Hippopotamus.*)

Baby (unhesitatingly). "MAM-MA."

22

VERY INTERESTING, IF ONE DID BUT KNOW A LITTLE MORE.

"And so Missus says, Mary, she says, tell me all about it, she says—and so I says, me, Marm?
I says—and with that, that's how it was, yer see."—"Lor!"

A WORD TO THE WISE.

Discerning Child (who has heard some remarks made by Papa). "ARE YOU OUR
NEW NURSE?"

Nurse. "YES, DEAR!"

Child. "WELL THEN, I'M ONE OF THOSE BOYS WHO CAN ONLY BE MANAGED WITH
KINDNESS—SO YOU HAD BETTER GET SOME SPONGE CAKES AND ORANGES AT ONCE!"

DOMESTIC BLISS.

Young Mother (*joyously*). . . . "THE DEAR LITTLE CREATURE IS GETTING ON SO NICELY; IT'S BEGINNING QUITE TO TAKE NOTICE."
First Mother of a Family (*blandly*). "OH! MY DEAR! THAT IS NOT TAKING NOTICE; IT'S ONLY THE WIND."
Second Ditto. . . . . "YOU SHOULD GIVE IT A LITTLE DILL WATER, DEAR. YOU WOULD FIND," &c., &c.
Third Ditto. . . . . "WELL, IF IT WAS MY CHILD, I SHOULD," &c., &c.
Fourth Ditto. . . . . "NOW, WHEN I WAS NURSING MY LITTLE GREGORY, I USED," &c., &c.
Fifth Ditto. . . . . "WELL NOW, I WOULD NOT FOR THE WORLD THAT A BABY OF MINE," &c., &c.
Sixth Ditto. . . . . "INDEED I HAVE KNOWN CHILDREN OBLIGED TO ENDURE THE MOST HORRIBLE AGONY," &c., &c.
Seventh Ditto. . . . . "DEPEND UPON IT, LOVE; AND YOU KNOW I HAVE HAD A LARGE FAMILY—AND IF YOU WILL BE
ADVISED BY ME," &c., &c. [*Young Mother becomes quite bewildered, and gives herself up to despair.*

THE PROGRESS OF SLANG.

"WHY, WHAT A PRETTY NEW FROCK ALFRED HAS!"
Prodigy (*who picks up everything so readily*). "AH, AINT IT A STUNNER!"

THRILLING DOMESTIC INCIDENT.

Master Alfred. "Don't Baby! You'll Spoil it. Leave go, Sir! Here, Nurse! He's Swallowing my New Watch."

"A VERY PRETTY QUARREL."

First Nurserymaid. "*Me go back, Miss! Oh dear no, not if I'm perfectly aware on it, Miss, which you might a' seen me henter the street fust, if you'd a' been looking straight before yer, Miss, So you're not a-goin' to turn me off the pavemint, if I stays here all day, beggin o' your pard—*"

Second Nurserymaid. "*Oh don't name it, Mum. I'm in no 'urry!*"

INGENIOUSLY PUT!

"Now Master Bobbie is going to be a good boy, and watch baby, while I go and Hask great, big, fierce, Mr. Soldier not to run away with Master Bobbie."

EASILY SATISFIED.

Fond Parent. "I DON'T CARE, MR. MEDIUM, ABOUT IT'S BEING HIGHLY FINISHED; BUT I SHOULD LIKE THE DEAR CHILD'S EXPRESSION PRESERVED."

SERVANTGALISM; AND

FINELADYISM.

First Elegant Mamma. "HOW SHOCKING THIS IS!—THE WAY NURSERYMAIDS NEGLECT THE CHILDREN!"

Second Do. "YES, DEAR! AND I DON'T SEE THAT ANYTHING CAN BE DONE. FOR WHAT WITH PARTIES, AND THE TIME ONE NATURALLY DEVOTES TO DRESSING, AND THE NUMEROUS CALLS ONE HAS TO MAKE, ONE CAN'T LOOK AFTER ONE'S OWN CHILDREN, YOU KNOW!"

P.O.C.—B

REMARKABLY CLEVER IDEA

Of Jones when he had to Run for the Doctor the other Morning at 2 a.m.

EARLY GENIUS.

" Bless 'is little 'art, he takes to it as natural as hanythink."

Old Lady.—"AH! I WAS JUST SUCH ANOTHER WHEN I WAS HER AGE."

Nurse. "DRAT THE CHILD! WHY CAN'T YER WALK?—YER MORE PLAGUE THAN ALL MY MONEY!"

DON'T BROIL YOUR BABIES!

BUT USE MR. PUNCH'S PATENT NURSEMAID'S BONNET-SCREEN. WARRANTED TO KEEP CHILDREN FROM THE SUN IN ANY CLIMATE.

THE MORNING CALL.

The Rev. Alban Rochet (High). "WON'T IT COME TO ITS PRIEST THEN ! ! !" *(Baby doesn't seem to see it.)*

A HINT TO MAMMAS.

First Nursemaid. "LAWK, MARIER! WHAT A BEE-UTIFLE GOWND!"
Second Do. "MY! JANE! HAINT IT?"
[*They contemplate the Gownd for about a quarter of an hour, and the Children
have the full benefit of the delicious North-East wind.*

Chorus (of nice young Ladies). "OH! OF ALL AND OF *ALL*, I NEVER! ISN'T **IT** THE
DARLINGEST, SWEETEST, PRETTIEST, LITTLE DEAR DARLING DARLING! OH! DID YOU EVER!!"
Solo (by horrid plain-spoken Boy). "HM! *I* THINK IT'S A NASTY, UGLY LITTLE BEAST, FOR
ALL THE WORLD LIKE A CAT OR A MONKEY." [*Sensation.*

THE LATEST IMPROVEMENT.

Jane. "Lawk, Jemima! Don't they look Bewtifle now they've got their Long Coats?"

Head Nurse (with much dignity). "MISS MARY! YOU SHALL NOT STIR YOUR TEA WITH THE SNUFFERS!—IT IS NOT LADY-LIKE, AND I AM QUITE SURE YOUR PAPA WOULD NOT APPROVE OF IT!"   [MISS MARY *howls awfully, and smashes tea-cup.*

NO ACCOUNTING FOR TASTE.

NURSE (in the distance). "*La, Miss Loo! whatever har you hat?*"
MISS LOO. "*I'm only painting Dolly's Face, to make her look like Ma of an afternoon.*"

TOO CLEVER BY HALF!

Little Girl. "OH, AUNTY, BABY'S MOUTH IS SO FUNNY—IT'S JUST LIKE YOURS BEFORE YOU GET OUT OF BED——NO, NOT ONE TOOTH!"

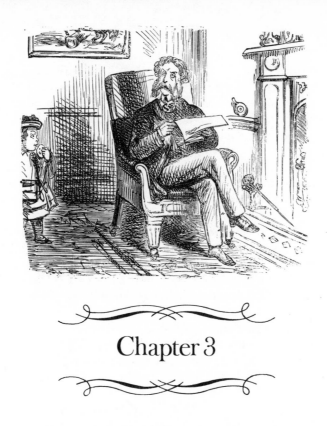

Chapter 3

PATERFAMILIAS

'Dear Father' of the mid-nineteenth century was, domestically speaking, rather a remote character. He was apt to be fierce and dictatorial, the result of having all the power in his hands and a wife without the status or experience to contradict him. The character portrayed by Charles Laughton in *The Barretts of Wimpole Street* was close to many of them.

For the wives, it was a case of bed and kitchen at the bottom end of the scale, bed and house hold administration in the middle, and bed and hostess at the top. Many fathers rated a bull pup more important than a baby, and their children soon learned to be out of the way when he came home, especially on Saturday nights. Middle class fathers were distinctly 'Old Testament', politically biased, pompous, and full of their own importance; it is the echo of them against which the young rebel today. Upper class fathers had other, and overriding, interests and only saw their children, arrayed in velvet, for a short time in the drawing-room after tea, when they listened to their reports on their educational progress.

Fathers were usually older then, the result of couples ensuring that, before they entered into matrimony, they were sufficiently secure, professionally and materially, to support a family which might well run into double figures. There was no Social

Security to fall back on. Promotion in the Services, professions and business was slow, and those who held the reins of power were not easily persuaded to loose their grip. 'Clever young pups' were not appreciated and experience was rated high.

Pram pushing and cradle rocking were absolutely taboo for fathers, and those who were suspected of indulging in such indignities were subjected to chaff at their clubs. 'True Courage' is the title given to the drawing of the top-hatted 'gent' walking along the pavement, holding his daughter by one hand and her doll in the other.

Sex was a problem for people of all classes. The poor did what came naturally. The rich had more chance of gaining experience, but were discovering that the ways of the Georgian days were very much in disfavour at Court. It was the middle classes. who suffered most. Sex was never mentioned in their homes and the young men and girls had little chance to learn. Papa was unapproachable. Mama, although she had had many children, knew surprisingly little. Queen Victoria, whose tribe numbered nine, crossed out in her old age, a reference to Lesbianism in the draft of a Bill, on the grounds that it was impossible. All the advice that a daughter might receive from the maternal quarter was to lie back, shut her eyes and put up with it.

During pregnancy, rich husbands would seek means of escape from intimacies of which they wanted no part. They might seize the opportunity to accept an invitation to hunt in Ireland, or join some minor campaign in India or one of the shores upon which the sun never set. Middle class fathers began to follow in the footsteps of their paragon, Prince Albert. He fussed about like a mother when his wife was 'expecting', ever ready to lift her from the sofa, ever ready with his arm to lead her. He kept the key to the nursery quarters on his watch chain and each evening checked that all his offspring were safely gathered in. He was reported to have assisted the nurse with childish tantrums, and was seen sliding and tobogganing with his young. This paternal tenderness, however, continued only until the child was old enough to answer back. Albert then climbed quickly onto his throne of dignity, for he could not bear to be contradicted. Thus he set the trend for the middle classes. Here is paterfamilias, on holiday at the seaside with his family, allowing his young to bury him up to the neck in sand. This, however, is deceptive bonhomie, as we also see him forcing his offspring to to drink spa water and parading his sons to endure the torture of the new-fangled shower-bath.

There are more human scenes — scenes which might well be set in the modern flat or suburban home — but here one suspects that the artist is allowing us to peep into his own home life, or that of a friend in the same line of business.

Our dear old Paterfamilias takes his Offspring to see the Pantomime. Unfortunately, "the Roads" (as the Cabman says) "is so Orribul bad and Slippy," that he is obliged to walk with his Darlings the greater part of the way home.

A PRETTY GENERAL OPINION.

Mr. Kiddlums. "WELL, ELIZABETH—I HOPE WE SHALL HAVE A PRIZE BABY SHOW
HERE—AND THEN—I FLATTER MYSELF— * * * * *"

TRUE COURAGE.

A NAUGHTY PAPA.

Young Mother. "JUST TAKE HIM, CHARLES; YOU'VE NO IDEA WHAT A WEIGHT HE IS!"

Paterfamilias. "MY DEAR GIRL, WHAT ARE YOU THINKING OF; TEN TO ONE I SHOULD DROP IT DOWN AND BREAK IT TO PIECES."

Edwin. "NOW, UPON MY LIFE, ANGELINA, THIS IS TOO BAD—NO BUTTONS AGAIN."

Angelina. "WELL, MY DEAR, IT'S OF NO USE FIDGETTING ME ABOUT IT. YOU MUST SPEAK TO ANN. YOU CAN'T EXPECT ME TO DO EVERYTHING."

Wife of your Bussum. "Oh! I don't want to interrupt you, dear. I only want some money for Baby's socks—and to know whether you will have the mutton cold or hashed."

Little Foot Page (unexpectedly). "Here's some Gentlemen, please, Sir!"

PLEASANT FOR "CHARLES DEAR."

Married Sister. "OH, CHARLES DEAR! NURSE IS NOT VERY WELL, AND AS I MUST STAY WITH BABY, WOULD YOU TAKE FREDDY AND THE TWO LITTLE ONES FOR A WALK, ONLY CARRY THEM OVER THE CROSSINGS, THAT'S A DEAR!"

Head of the Family. "FOR WHAT WE ARE GOING TO RECEIVE, MAKE US TRULY THANKFUL.—HEM! COLD MUTTON AGAIN!"

Wife of the Bussum. "AND A VERY GOOD DINNER TOO, ALEXANDER. SOMEBODY MUST BE ECONOMICAL. PEOPLE CAN'T EXPECT TO HAVE *RICHMOND* AND *GREENWICH* DINNERS OUT OF THE LITTLE HOUSEKEEPING MONEY *I* HAVE."

WHILE THEY ARE AT SCARBOROUGH, PATERFAMILIAS THINKS HIS LITTLE ONES OUGHT TO LOSE NO
OPPORTUNITY OF DRINKING THE WATERS!

" It was a pleasant thing to walk on the beach, and see how amiably that great, good-natured
fellow, Paterfamilias, was buried alive by the little ones."—*Extract from Letter*.

42

ANOTHER BIT FROM THE MINING DISTRICTS.

"Martha, wast 'e done wi' the Milk?"
"Geen it to the Shild."
"Dang the Shild, thee should ha' geen it to th' Bull Pup!"

ANSWER TO KIND INQUIRIES.

Poor Curate. "Thank you—yes—Mrs. Drudgett and the twins are going on nicely."

THE WEDDING DAY—FIRST ANNIVERSARY.

PRESENTS—BEAUTIFUL BOUQUET OF FLOWERS FROM COVENT GARDEN, AND SUCH
A LOVELY BRACELET ! !

THE WEDDING DAY—FOURTEENTH ANNIVERSARY.

PRESENTS—BEAUTIFUL BUNDLE OF ASPARAGUS FROM COVENT GARDEN, AND THE NICEST
DOUBLE PERAMBULATOR IN THE WORLD ! !

44

Chapter 4

TOYS AND PASTIMES

Yesterday's children made their own amusements. Except for the occasional outing to the pantomime or the circus, the fair or an exhibition, parents made little attempt to amuse their offspring. Organised games were rare.

Nature provided a recurring programme of fun — skating and snowballing in the winter, flowers in the spring, fishing and bathing in the summer, 'conkers' and berry-picking in the autumn. For the rest children made many of their own toys. The essentials for bows and arrows and pea-shooters were cut from the trees. Boats were carved from lumps of wood — George V's favourite toy when a boy was a sailing ship fashioned by a man-servant at Sandringham. It was not until the prosperous days of 1865 that *Punch* featured a shop devoted entirely to toys and games, and even then parents had to be careful that their purchases were suitable for children to play with on Sundays.

The years saw crazes for toys come and go, and the artists walking along London's streets noted them — sometimes to their discomfort. Balls tied to the end of pieces of string whizzed round old ladies' heads, thoroughly upsetting their sedate progress. Boys in horrific masks terrified little girls and babies. Business men were forced to duck as they made their way through a game of battledore and shuttlecock. Giant Spiders were hawked by street vendors for a penny each. Spinning tops become a menace to the feet especially those of the portly whose waistcoats prevented a close watch being kept on the pavement, and penny whistles were as great a nuisance as the italian organ grinders. Treasured pea-shooters could come to an untimely end when some unsuspecting passer-by received a pea in the ear.

Girls skipped and bowled their wooden hoops — metal ones being reserved for boys. With the Crimean War and the Volunteer Movement the sales of wooden soldiers and military equipment boomed. Prince Arthur, godson of the Duke of Wellington and later Duke of Connaught, had a trumpet which shattered the peace of Windsor and had at length, to be removed forcibly. Those to whom none of this was available could always resort to breaking Aunt Sally's nose as a convenient way of letting of steam.

Riding was more of a necessary accomplishment than a pastime, and the children of the rich were out in the hunting field as soon as their legs could grip a saddle. For boys, fishing was a favourite pastime throughout the class and financial range. Football had not yet 'arrived'; at the century's opening, Joseph Strutt wrote that, though the game had formerly been much in vogue with the common people, it had fallen into disrepute. It was not until the end of the period we are dealing with that order emerged from the chaos of opinion as to whether hands or feet should be used. Firm rules were laid down around 1866. Thereafter Rugby and Association took over the hearts and minds of all the boys.

Boxing, on the other hand, came in with a punch. The big fights attracted much attention and Papa invited the local champion, dubbed 'the professor', to attend the schoolroom; even the girls were allowed to sample the gloves. Cricket had been played for a long time, but it was not until the railways made it possible for touring sides to move easily about the country that it gained popular appeal.

Perhaps it would appear that yesterday's children were poorly served compared with those of a century later. Yet there is bliss on the face of the little girl who sits on the curb and blows her penny whistle. To the young of all ages fun is a constant value, and they will always find the means of making it.

Police Constable (to Boy). "NOW THEN, OFF WITH THAT HOOP! OR I'LL PRECIOUS SOON HELP YOU!"
Lady (who imagines the observation is addressed to her). "WHAT A MONSTER!"   [*Lifts up the Crinoline, and hurries off.*

47

THE HORRORS OF WAR.

First Newmarket Boy. "Awful work this, Bill. We're a goin' to war with Roosia!"
Second Ditto. "Well, wot odds?"
First Ditto. "Wot odds? Why, there won't be no Hemperor's Cup next year, that's all!"

SOMETHING LIKE SPORT.

Jolly Angler. "Hooray, Tom! I've got one—and my word! Didn't he pull?"

"I'LL PUNCH YOUR 'EAD, DIRECTLY, IF YOU DON'T LEAVE ORFF. HOW DO YER THINK THE
WHAT'S-A-NAMES 'LL BITE, IF YOU KEEP ON A SPLASHIN' LIKE THAT?"

A SHOCKING YOUNG LADY INDEED!

Emily (*betrothed to Charles*). "OH, CHARLES, ISN'T IT FUN? I'VE BEATEN ARTHUR AND JULIA, AND I'VE BROKE AUNT SALLY'S
NOSE SEVEN TIMES!"

MOST UNACCOUNTABLE.

"CONFOUND THAT URCHIN, HERE HAVE I BEEN FLOGGING AWAY ALL DAY, AND NOT EVEN CAUGHT SO MUCH AS A TITTLEBAT."

"Oh !! Look'ee here, Sir, here's a warm long enough to last you a fortnight."

VAULTING AMBITION.

"Now, then, Charity—Higher! You don't call that a Back!"

Georgina. "Why, what's the matter with my Little Poppet?"
Little Poppet. "Oh, Aunty dear, Walter can't find his Stumps, so he is making a Wicket of my best Doll!"

Young Lady. "NOW THEN, GIRLS, JUST LET ME——"

Girl (interrupting, before the word "PASS" *can escape the lips of the fair Pedestrian).* "OH! IT AIN'T NO USE YOUR TRYING A TURN, MISS. THERE ISN'T ABOVE ROOM TO TAKE IN BETSY SIMMONS."

NOTHING LIKE HORSE EXERCISE.

"Now, Aunt! Touch him with your left heel, and let's have a trot!"

A SERIOUS JOKE.

Mamma (whose darling is undecided whether to choose a Noah's Ark or a Box of Wooden Animals). "WHICH DO YOU RECOMMEND, MR. CANTWELL?"

Mr. C. "WELL, MUM, YOU SEE NOAH BEIN' MENTIONED IN 'OLY WRIT, WE ALWAYS RECKONS THE HARK 'AS THE ADVANTAGE OF BEIN' A SUNDAY TOY, MUM!!"

Philanthropist. "WHAT NOW, MY MAN?"
Street Boy. "THEY'VE BEEN AND GONE AND SPIKED MY PEASHOOTER

A REHEARSAL!

"Now, don't you 'urry the Handanty (*Andante*) this time,
young feller!"

FLY-DRESSING IN THE HOLIDAYS.

"I say, Pug, just give me two or three of your Eyelashes, to finish off this Black Palmer, there's a good Girl."

WHILE THEY ARE ABOUT IT, THE AUTHORITIES HAD BETTER SEND A FEW SPECIAL CONSTABLES DOWN TO BRIGHTON, WHERE THEY ARE QUITE AS FUNNY AS THEY ARE AT GUILDFORD ON GUY FAWKES DAY—INDEED THE FUN SOMETIMES REACHES TO THE PITCH OF AN IDLE YOUNG RUFFIAN SENDING A CHILD INTO CONVULSIONS WITH A HIDEOUS MASK!

THE SENSATION BALL!

THE LATEST PLEASANTRY IN THE PUBLIC STREETS.

Alfred. "OH, IF YOU PLEASE, UNCLE, WE WANT TO PLAY AT BEING WILLIAM TELL; WILL YOU BE SO KIND AS TO STAND WITH THE APPLE ON YOUR HEAD?"

USEFUL, IF NOT ORNAMENTAL.

Master Alfred (an ingenious boy). "LOOK HERE, WALTER! SEE WHAT A JOLLY TARGET OLD AUNT BETSY'S ROUND HAT MAKES."

WE SHOULD THINK IT DID!

Clara. "MAMMA, DEAR! I WISH YOU WOULD SPEAK TO GEORGE: HE WILL KEEP SPINNING FREDDY'S NASTY GREAT HUMMING-TOP IN MY AQUARIUM, AND IT DOES SO FRIGHTEN THE MINNOWS!"

ALARMING EPIDEMIC—THE WHISTLEPHOBIA.

THE ANIMATED EGG.

"Oh, Ma! ain't this a Whacking Snowball? and Cousin Charley is inside!"

LATE FROM THE NURSERY.

Governess. "Now, Frank, you must put your Drum down, if you are going to say your Prayers."

Frank. "Oh, do let me wear it, please; I'll pomise not to think about it."

59

ONLY A PENNY! A SENSIBLE AND INGENIOUS TOY FOR CHILDREN.

Old Gent. "CONFOUND THE BOYS AND THEIR TOPS! WHERE ARE THE POLICE?"

Chapter 5

EDUCATIONAL SUPPLEMENT

'Larning' was restricted to the privileged few in the first half of the nineteenth century. Those who advocated general education were regarded as 'high brows' or trouble-makers despite the obvious dangers of a fast increasing population and the threat to public safety that ignorance could constitute. "An objection to educating working people was part of the general philosophy of the governing world. The working classes were regarded as people to be kept out of mischief rather than people with faculties and characters to be encouraged and developed. They were to have just so much instruction as would make them useful work-people."[1]

The rich feared education because they depended for their comfort upon the subservience of the poor. Industrialists tolerated only a degree of instruction sufficient to enable their employees to carry out their work more efficiently. This was referred to as 'a training in industry and piety', and did not include dangerous accomplishments such as reading and writing. The Established Church wished to get a universal grip on education and thus to impregnate the souls of the pupils while they were very young. Quite naturally, other sects were in violent opposition to this. Employers of children and poor parents were, both for differing reasons, in opposition to attendance at school. The employers would lose cheap labour, and the parents the

[1] *The Town and Country Labourer.* By J.L. and B. Hammond.

income of their offspring upon which they depended to meet the weekly expenses. So sad little Tommy and Mary had to wait a long time before they received the chance to learn the alphabet and elementary mathematics. In 1841 in Oldham and Ashton, with a population of over one hundred thousand, there was not a single public day school for the children of the poor.

There were many reformers who realised the importance of schooling. An important step came in 1809 with the founding of the National Society for the promoting of the education of the poor in the principles of the Established Church. There were other pioneers, the British and Foreign School Society, the Volunteer School Society, the Congregational Board of Education, the Home and Colonial Society and the Ragged School Union. Even so it was not until five years before the accession of Queen Victoria that the first Government grant was given for public education — a mere twenty thousand pounds, to be confined to the erection of school buildings. In 1839 Lord Melbourne's Government increased this to thirty-nine thousand pounds, but the original intention to establish a State normal school or training college as the foundation of a national system of education, was abandoned owing to religious difficulties. It seemed that those who could not get their own way were prepared to sacrifice schooling altogether rather than give ground. In 1850 *Punch* summed up the position in a sketch:

A JUVENILE TEACHER ON EDUCATION

Interlocutors.—LITTLE BOY AND MIDDLE-AGED GENTLEMAN.

We beg to call the attention of the House of Commons to the following interesting dialogue:—

Little Boy. Please Papa, what are you reading, Papa?

Middle-aged Gentleman. The speeches in Parliament, my little man; all about educating the millions of poor little boys and girls who can't read and write, and don't know their A, B, C, nor the difference between right and wrong.

Little Boy. Why don't their Papas and Mammas have them taught, Papa?

Middle-aged Gentleman. My dear, because they have no kind, good, Papas and Mammas like you. Some of their parents are too poor, and some too careless and indifferent.

Little Boy. Then Papa, why doesn't the QUEEN order them to be sent to school?

Middle-aged Gentleman. Ha! her MAJESTY would be only too happy, if she could; but Parliament can't agree to let her.

Little Boy. Why not, Papa?

Middle-aged Gentleman. Why, you see, my dear, Parliament is made up of gentlemen that belong to different religions, and not one of them, except a few, will vote for any school unless his own religion is taught in it. So the poor little girls and boys can't be taught anything because the sects can't settle their differences.

Little Boy. What differences, Papa?

Middle-aged Gentleman. I can't explain them to you. You couldn't understand them. They don't signify to little boys of your age.

Little Boy. Then, Papa, what do they signify to the poor little boys and girls?

Middle-aged Gentleman. Eh?—why—a—just so—that is—never mind. You'll know one of these days.

Little Boy. But what becomes of the poor boys and girls, Papa?

Middle-aged Gentleman. Why, they plunder and steal, and then they are taken up, and imprisoned and whipped, and by-and-by transported, and at last some of them hanged— all because they haven't been taught their duty like you, and know no better.

Little Boy. How cruel! If they don't know better, whose fault is it, Papa?

Middle-aged Gentleman. Nobody's in particular. It is because Society can't agree.

Little Boy. Who is Society, Papa?

Middle-aged Gentleman. Society—eh? —why—oh! Everybody, my boy.

Little Boy. Then I think, Papa, it is the fault of Everybody, and I think Everybody is very wicked, and will never be happy till he can make his mind up, and send the poor children to school.

Middle-aged Gentleman. 'Pon my word, my little boy, I believe you are right.

As "the fat years of mid-Victorian prosperity" approached, it became obvious that something had to be done, and who better to wave the flag than Prince Albert the Consort, the master-mind behind Wellington College? Highly educated himself, a product of Bonn University, he had been a benefactor of the schools on the royal estates. On 22nd June 1857 he spoke at the opening of the Conference on National Education at Willis's Rooms. His speech (less the final appeal to the Almighty to lend a hand) is quoted verbatim. Not only is it one of the finest contemporary summaries of the problem of education, but reveals his knowledge and grasp of the subject. He had to be careful — and he knew it — for priests and politicians, parents and employers, were on the watch to ensure that he did not interfere with their interests:

"GENTLEMEN,—

We have met to-day in the sacred cause of Education—of National Education. This word, which means no less than the moral and intellectual development of the rising generation, and, therefore, the national welfare, is well calculated to engross our minds, and opens a question worthy of a nation's deepest interest and most anxious consideration. Gentlemen, the nation is alive to its importance, and our presence here to-day gives further evidence (if such evidence were needed) of its anxiety to give it that consideration. Looking to former times, we find that our forefathers, with their wonted piety and paternal care, had established a system of national education, based upon the parish organisation, and forming part of parish life, which met the wants of their day, and had in it a certain unit and completeness which we may well envy at the present moment. But in the progress of time our wants have outstripped that system, and the condition of the country has so completely changed, even within these last fifty years, that the old parochial division is no longer adequate for the present population.

This has increased during that period in England and Wales from, in round numbers, 9,000,000 to 18,000,000, and, where there formerly existed comparatively small towns and villages, we now see mighty cities, like Liverpool, Manchester, Hull, Leeds, Birmingham, and others, with their hundreds of thousands, springing up almost, as it were, by enchantment; London having increased to nearly two and a half million of souls, and the factory district of Lancashire alone having aggregated a population of nearly 3,000,000 within a radius of thirty miles. This change could not escape the watchful eye of a patriotic public; but how to provide the means of satisfying the new wants could not be a matter of easy solution. While zeal for the public good, a fervent religious spirit, and true philanthropy are qualities eminently distinguishing our countrymen, the love of liberty, and an aversion from being controlled by the power of the State in matters nearest to their hearts, are feelings which will always most powerfully influence them in action. Thus the common object has been contemplated from the most different points of view, and pursued often upon antagonistic principles. Some have sought the aid of Government, others that of the Church to which they belong; some have declared it to be the duty of the State to provide elementary instruction for the people at large, others have seen in the State interference a check to the spontaneous exertions of the people themselves, and an interference with self-government; some, again, have advocated a plan of compulsory education based upon local self-government, and others the voluntary system in its widest development. While these have been some of the political subjects of difference, those in the religious field have not been less marked and potent. We find, on the one hand, the wish to see secular and religious instruction separated, and the former recognized as an innate and inherent right, to which each member of society has a claim, and which ought not to be denied to him if he refuses to take along with it the inculcation of a particular dogma to which he objects as unsound; while we see, on the other hand, the doctrine asserted, that no education can be sound which does not rest on religious instruction, and that religious truth is too sacred to be modified and tampered with, even in its minutest deductions, for the sake of procuring a general agreement.

"Gentlemen, if these differences were to have been discussed here to-day, I should not have been able to respond to your invitation to take the chair, as I should have thought it inconsistent with the position which I occupy, and with the duty which I owe to the Queen and the country at large. I see those here before me who have taken a leading part in these important discussions, and I am happy to meet them upon a neutral gound; happy to find that there is a neutral ground upon which their varied talents and abilities can be brought to bear in communion upon the common object; and proud and grateful to them that they should have allowed me to preside over them for the purpose of working together in the common vineyard. I feel certain that the greatest benefit must arise to the cause we have all so much at heart by the mere free exchange of your thoughts and various experience. You may well be proud, gentlemen, of the results hitherto achieved by your rival efforts, and may point to the fact that, since the beginning of the century, while the population has doubled itself, the number of schools, both public and private, has been multiplied fourteen times. In 1801 there were in England and Wales, of public schools, 2876; of private schools, 487—total, 3363. In 1851 (the year of the census) there were in England and Wales, of public schools, 15,518; of private schools, 30,524—total 46,042; giving instruction in all to 2,144,378 scholars; of whom 1,422,982 belong to public schools, and 721,396 to the private schools. The rate of progress is further illustrated by statistics which show that in 1818 the proportion of day-scholars to the population was 1 in 17; in 1833, 1 in 11; and 1851, 1 in 8. These are great results, although I hope they may only be received as instalments of what has yet to be done. But what must be your feelings when you reflect upon the fact, the inquiry into which has brought us together, that this great boon thus obtained for the mass of the people, and which is freely offered to them, should have been only partially accepted, and, upon the whole, so insufficiently applied as to render its use almost valueless! We are told that, the total population in England and Wales of children between the ages of 3 and 15 being estimated at 4,908,696, only 2,046,848 attend school at all, while 2,861,848 receive no instruction whatever. At the same time an analysis of the scholars with reference to the length of time allowed for their school tuition, shows that 42 per cent. of them have been at school for less than one year, 22 per cent. during one year, 15 per cent. during two years, 9 per cent. during three years, 5 per cent. during four years, and 4 per cent. during five years. Therefore, out of the two millions of scholars alluded to, more than one million and a half remain only two years at school. I leave it to you to judge what the results of such an education can be. I find further that of these two millions of children attending school only about 600,000 are above the age of nine.

"Gentlemen, these are startling facts, which render it evident that no extension of the means of education will be of any avail unless this evil, which lies at the root of the whole question, be removed, and that it is high time that the country should become thoroughly awake to its existence, and prepared to meet it energetically. To impress this upon the public mind is the object of our conference. Public opinion is the powerful lever which in these days moves a people for good and for evil, and to public opinion we must therefore appeal if we would achieve any lasting and beneficial results. You, gentlemen, will richly add to the services which you have already rendered to the noble cause if you will prepare public opinion by your inquiry into this state of things, and by discussing in your sections the causes of it as well as the remedies which may lie within our reach. This will be no easy matter; but even if your labours should not result in the adoption of any immediate practical steps, you will have done great good in preparing for them. It will probably happen that, in this instance as in most others, the cause which produces the evil will be more easily detected than its remedy, and yet a just appreciation of the former must ever be the first and essential condition for the discovery of the latter. You will probably trace the cause of our social condition to a state of ignorance and lethargic indifference on the subject among parents generally; but the root of the evil will, I suspect, be found to extend into that field on which the political economist exercises his activity— I mean the labour market—demand and supply. To dissipate that ignorance and rouse from that lethargy may be difficult; but with the united and earnest efforts of all who are the friends of the working classes it ought, after all, to be only a question of time. What measures can be brought to bear upon the other root of the evil is a more delicate question, and will require the nicest care in handling, for there you cut into the very quick of the working man's condition. His children are not only his offspring, to be reared for a future independent position, but they constitute part of his productive power, and work with him for the staff of life; the daughters especially are the handmaids of the house, the assistants of the mother, the nurses of the younger children, the aged, and the sick. To deprive the labouring family of their help would be almost to paralyse its domestic existence. On the other hand, carefully collected statistics reveal to us the fact, that, while about 600,000 children between the ages of 3 and 15 are absent from school, but known to be employed, no less than 2,200,000 are not at schools, whose absence cannot be traced to any ascertained employment or other legitimate cause. You will have to work, then, upon the minds and hearts of the parents, to place before them the irreparable mischief which they inflict upon those who are intrusted to their care by keeping them from the light of knowledge, to bring home to their conviction that it is their duty to exert themselves for their children's education, bearing in mind at the same time that it is not only their most sacred duty, but also their highest privilege."

The answer was not, however, to be found in the Prince's lifetime. It came with William Edward Forster's Elementary Education Act of 1870. Schooling became compulsory and universal, and Britain became a nation all the members of which had the opportunity to learn to read and to write.

Although *Punch*, in its columns, waged a continuing fight to obtain better schooling for the young in need of it, there were comparatively few drawings touching on education. One notable lack was of scenes inside the public schools and of the life of boys who underwent a baptism such as Tom Brown endured at Rugby. One can only surmise that either the contributors had not attended such establishments, or, if they had, wished the memory to lie dormant. There were, however, occasional attacks on bullying and sadism at such schools, as there was pungent criticism of the 'private' schools, unchecked and uninspected, to which unkindly parents sent boys of whom they wished to be rid. Here the object was to extract as much profit as possible from the unhappy pupils, and we glimpse a scene at 'Mr. Swindle's' academy, the boys being dosed with cod liver oil to make them appear well fed before they returned to their homes for Christmas.

The most frequent jokes in this field concerned the trend for higher education which blossomed in the 1850s and 1860s. Thus we see child prodigies producing items of advanced knowledge, while their parents regard them with astonishment. It was a fast changing world.

Old Gentleman. "WELL, WALTER, I SUPPOSE YOU HAVE GOT INTO LATIN AND GREEK AT SCHOOL BY THIS TIME, EH?"

Juvenile. "OH YES, SIR; I HAVE JUST FINISHED XENOPHON AND THUCYDIDES, AND AM NOW IN EURIPIDES. BY THE WAY, SIR, HOW WOULD YOU RENDER THE PASSAGE BEGINNING κακῶς πέπρακται πανταχῆ?"

Old Gentleman. "AHEM! HEY?—WHAT?—AHEM! HERE, RUGGLES! BRING ANOTHER BOTTLE OF CLARET, AND—EH?—WHAT? WALTER, I THINK YOU HAD BETTER JOIN THE LADIES."

EDUCATION FOR THE MIDDLE CLASSES.

Scene—*Toy-Shop.* *Enter highly educated Youth of Twelve.*

"Oh, I want some Toy, or conjuring Trick, or something that would do for an old Gentleman of Fifty or thereabouts; my Grandfather, in point of fact,—you know the kind of thing, I dessay."

Papa. "Well, Lucy, what has Miss Trimmer set you to do for To-morrow?"

Lucy. "Oh, Papa, dear, it's on Pneumatics in relation to—but you really *wouldn't* understand it, if I told you."

CONSIDERATE—VERY!

Master George (alluding to the New Governess, who happened to be within hearing). "CROSS, DISAGREEABLE OLD THING, I CALL HER!"
Miss Caroline. "OH, GEORGY! BUT WE OUGHT TO GIVE WAY TO HER; RECOLLECT, DEAR, SHE'S A VERY AWKWARD AGE!"

KENSINGTON GARDENS. A POSER FOR PAPA.

"LA! PA, DEAR!—WHAT IS THE MEANING OF 'KŒLRUTERIA PANICULATA;' AND WHY
SHOULD SUCH A LITTLE TREE HAVE SUCH A VERY LONG NAME?"

"THE EDUCATIONAL QUESTION."

"BETWEEN TWO STOOLS HE COMES TO THE GROUND"—*Old Proverb.*

A PRODIGIOUS NUISANCE.

Learned (but otherwise highly objectionable) Child (loq.) "Oh, Mamma, Dear! What do you think? I asked Mr. —— and Miss —— to name some of the Remarkable Events from the Year 700 to the Year 600 B.C., and they couldn't. But *I* can—and—The Second Messenian War commenced; and—the Poet Tyrtæus flourished; Byzantium was founded by the Inhabitants of Megara; Draco gave Laws to Athens; Terpander of Lesbos, the Musician and Poet; Thales of Miletus, the Philosopher; Alcæus and Sappho, the Poets, flourished; and Nebuchadnez——"

[*Sensation from right and left, during which the Voice of Child is happily drowned.*

CONDESCENDING.

Master Tom (going back to School, to Fellow Passenger). "If you'd like to Smoke, you know, Gov'nour, don't you mind me, I rather like it!"

MIDDLE-CLASS EDUCATION.

MR. SWINDLE'S ONLY METHOD OF PREPARATION FOR THE CHRISTMAS EXAMINATION.

ACADEMIC COSTUME.

Dr. Bear. "PUT ON YOUR GOWN, SIR."
Undergraduate. "GOT IT ON, SIR."

Fond Mother. "Why, he doesn't write very well yet, but he gets on nicely with his spelling. Come, Alexander, what does D. O. G. spell?"

Infant Prodigy (*with extraordinary quickness*). "Cat!"

OH, BY ALL MEANS REVISE THE CODE!

Teacher (*certificated*). "'Enery, 'Enery! Where's yer 'ands?"

VERY PARTICULAR.

First Railway Porter. "What does he say, Bill?"
Second Ditto. "Why he says he must have a Compartment to hisself, because he can't get on without his Smoke!"

LATE FROM THE SCHOOL-ROOM.

Minnie. "I AM READING SUCH A PRETTY TALE."
Governess. "YOU MUST SAY NARRATIVE, MINNIE—NOT TALE!"
Minnie. "YES, MA'AM; AND DO JUST LOOK AT MUFF, HOW HE'S WAGGING HIS NARRATIVE!"

Old Gentleman (who has a sensitive ear for Grammar). "*My dears, there's your Mother calling you.*"
Wild Boy of the West. "*O, her ain't a callin' o' we; us don't belong to she.*"

FIRST DAY AT SCHOOL.

PAPA. "*Well, Sissy, how do you like School?*"
SISSY. "*Oh! So muts.*"
PAPA. "*That's right.   Now tell me all you have learnt to-day.*"
SISSY. "*I've learnt the names of all the little boys!*"

A PLEASANT KIND OF UNCLE.

SCENE—*Inside a Cab. UNCLE on back seat. Two nice boys on front seat.*

Uncle. "NOW, REGINALD, LOOK OVER MY HEAD, AND TELL ME THE NUMBER OF THIS CAB."
Reginald (slowly). "ONE, SIX, SIX, EIGHT."
Uncle (sternly). "HOW DARE YOU, SIR? SAY SIXTEEN HUNDRED AND SIXTY-EIGHT. NOW, JAMES. WHAT IMPORTANT EVENTS IN ENGLISH HISTORY HAPPENED IN 1688?"
[*The Boys think they might as well not be out for a Cheerful Holiday.*

THE FAGGING SYSTEM.—TRIUMPH OF MIND OVER MATTER.

Old Gent. "AND PRAY WHO IS YOUR FRIEND WITH THE COFFEE POT?"
Small Boy. "THAT? OH! HE'S MY FAG—HE GETS ME MY BREAKFAST AND SUCH LIKE, BUT I ALWAYS LEAVE HIM SOME CRUMPETS—AND—*NEVER BULLY HIM!*"

EDUCATIONAL.

SCHOOL-TEACHER. "*Now, Jeremiah Muzzles, spell Gold.*"
JEREMIAH (rather backward for his age). "*G–O–L–D.*"
SCHOOL-TEACHER. "*Right. What is Gold?*"
JEREMIAH. "*Doan't Knoah.*"

SCHOOL-TEACHER (exhibiting chain and eye-glass). "*Why, what is this, Sir?*"
JEREMIAH. "*Brass, Teacher!*"
[JEREMIAH "*stood 'corrected'*" immediately afterwards.

SHARP SHOE-BLACK. "*I say, Bill, what's the last Letter but one of the Alphabet?*"
BILL. "*Y.*"
SHARP SHOE BLACK. "*'Cos I wants to know, Stoopid.*"

INCORRIGIBLE.

Clerical Examiner. "WHAT IS YOUR NAME?"
Incorrigible. "BILER, SIR."
Clerical Examiner. "WHO GAVE YOU THAT NAME?"
Incorrigible. "THE *BOYS IN OUR COURT*, SIR."

EDUCATION IN THE MINING DISTRICTS.

Jemoimer. "BIST THOU A GOIN TO SKULE, ELOYZA?"
Eloyza. "NOT HI, JEMOIMER. THEY GID US TEA AND BUNS LARST WEEK, AND WE SHA'T HAN NO MOORE TILL CUM CRISMUS; SO MUTHER SAYS AS HOW IT AIN'T NO USE."

THE EXHAUSTED STUDENT.

Fond Parient. "BLESS HIS HEART—ALWAYS STUDYING! READ HIMSELF ASLEEP—GEOGRAPHY NOW, OR SOMETHING OF THAT SORT, I'LL BE BOUND!"

[*No. It's the Cookery Book.*

PRACTICAL SCIENCE.

Grandmamma. "WELL, CHARLEY, AND WHAT HAVE YOU BEEN LEARNING, TO-DAY?"

Charley. "PNEUMATICS, GRAN'MA!—AND I CAN TELL YOU SUCH A DODGE!—IF I WAS TO PUT YOU UNDER A GLASS RECEIVER, AND EXHAUST THE AIR, ALL YOUR WRINKLES WOULD COME OUT AS SMOOTH AS GRANDPAPA'S HEAD!"

THE GREAT EXHIBITION.—THE DIVING-DRESS DEPARTMENT.

IN THE FOREGROUND IS A TROUBLESOME BOY (WHO HAS STRAYED FROM HIS
PARTY) AND COME SUDDENLY UPON THE FIGURE. HE IS HURRYING AWAY—FEAR
DEPICTED ON HIS COUNTENANCE.

THE COMET.

Master Tom. "I SAY, GRAN'MA, THIS IS A BAD JOB ABOUT THE COMET!"

Gran'ma. "GOOD GRACIOUS! WHAT'S THE MATTER?"

Master Tom. "WHY, HERE'S A LETTER IN THE PAPER SAYS:—'The particles of the tail, if thrown out from the head, having only, as before, the same rate of orbital motion as the head, and having larger and larger orbits to describe, the further they are removed from the head will necessarily fall further and further behind as they recede from the comet, and thus form a curve independently of a resisting medium;' AND THAT 'the panic-allaying doctrine of the tenuity of cometic nuclei cannot be maintained from the mere fact of their translucency.'"

[GRAN'MA *collapses.*

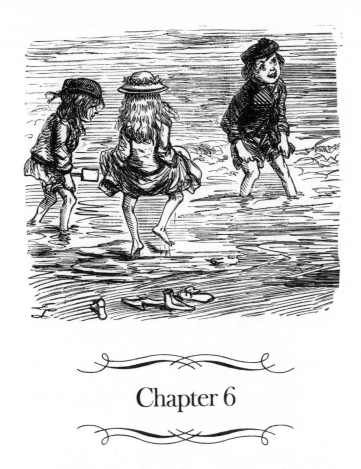

Chapter 6

BESIDE THE SEASIDE

King George III was largely responsible for the British delight in salt water bathing and holidays by the sea. He 'made' Weymouth, visiting it every summer from 1789 to 1805, and other south coast resorts were quick to court his patronage. Fanny Burney wrote: "The King bathes, and with great success; a machine follows the Royal one into the sea, filled with fiddlers who play 'God save the King' as His Majesty takes his plunge." There was nothing but the sea at Weymouth, however, as one of his ladies remarked, and getting up at six o'clock in the morning to watch Papa bathing was not very exciting for the Princesses.

The time had not yet come for universal enjoyment of the sea. Transport to the coast was slow and difficult and the middle classes had not yet reached the status when they could close their businesses and emigrate *en famille* for summer holidays. Holidays for the poor were simply not considered and a century was to pass before the first Holiday Homes were built for the benefit of the children who needed a change most, those from the big cities, who were thus able to fill their lungs with the "briny" breeze and put some colour in their cheeks.

For the aristocracy, vacations meant, wars permitting, the Grand Tour of Europe, Florence, Rome, Naples and Paris were on the itinerary. Lady Dorothy Nevill tells how she visited Bavaria in the 1830s. Although she was only nine, she rode most of the way to Munich on her pony. The family cavalcade consisted of four carriages and six saddle horses.

George IV did for Brighton what his father had done for Weymouth, but as Prince of Wales and Regent his tastes were more inclined to late night festivities and high living than plunging into cold water. His niece, Princess Victoria, spent her childhood holidays at resorts such as Ramsgate, Hastings and St. Leonards, but her mother would not allow her to bathe. Victoria's first plunge came in 1847, when she was twenty-eight. She had but recently bought the Osborne estate in the Isle of Wight and had the advantage of a private beach. A vast bathing machine, with a curtained verandah, took her out into the waves. She wrote in her diary: "I thought it delightful till I put my head under the water, when I thought I should be stifled."

PICKED UP FROM THE BEACH.

Old Salt (who has got Sixpence apiece out of the Children). " THERE, MY DEARS, YOU 'VE GOT A KITTEN FOR A SHILLUN' AS HAD OUGHT TO A BIN SEVIN AND SIX-PENCE AT LEAST ; AND IF YOU 'LL MEET ME HERE TO-MORRER AT THE SAME TIME, YOU SHALL HAVE SUCH A BOAT FOR A HALF-A-CROWN AS YOU COULDN'T GET AT A SHOP FOR FIVE BOB ! "

What the Queen could do, so could her people, and the new railways made everything simple. Those of restricted means took cheap day trips to the coast. The better off went to Ramsgate, Margate or Scarborough for a fortnight. Hotels, and lodging houses in long rows, sprung up in villages which soon became towns. It was all such an adventure. Mama simply had no idea how to pack only the necessities, and trunk after trunk was piled on the cab taking the family to the station. Then came the argument with the landlady over terms, and the search that no obnoxious insects were resident in the beds. Fish was the staple diet — many people did not know how newly caught, off-shore fish tasted; by the time the catches reached the big inland cities, they were anything but fresh. Then there were new tastes, such as crabs and shrimps. The local fishermen found themselves with a new and eager market and made the early morning hideous as they shouted their wares along the front. The retired ones would regale the younger generation with stirring, but dubious, tales of their adventures at sea and, with questionable deals over nautical toys, extract the holiday money from the children's pockets.

Papa and Mamma had a hearty respect for the sea and refused to enter it. Neither had they any intention of appearing in scanty apparel before the public gaze — there had been no such goings-on when they were young. They contented themselves with a stroll along the esplanade, a climb up the cliff path, an exploration of the gardens or a sail round the bay. Even their young were chary of the water at first, for their introduction to submersion was a stout and bawdy bathing woman, who seized them from the steps of the bathing machine and promptly ducked them with sadistic delight.

Girls bathing was the talk of the time. Precautions against any Peeping Tom catching a glimpse of their contours were exaggerated. An awning shrouded the steps of their bathing machines, and young men who loitered in the area were the object of black looks and the arrows of *Punch's* artists.

The two horrors of parents on holiday were the sun and the exposure of the human body. The sun was not allowed to tan the skin — it was considered dangerous to health — and we see Mama shading her offspring by wearing a hat with a very wide brim. As for the body, nothing more revealing than a baby's bottom was seen on the shore. Children old enough to bathe were garbed in a vestment like unto a pair of combinations stretching down to their ankles. Nudity then was considered an advanced, and wicked, attachment to straight sex, and many married couples never saw one another in the altogether. The bare bosoms of the eighteenth century were but a shameful memory and the sanctity of dear Prince Albert blanketed the land. There was therefore considerable comment when a naked, and shapely, young woman in marble appeared in the American Section of the Great International Exhibition of 1851. Despite many protests and expressions of disapproval, she was under continual inspection from an eager crowd.

Queen Victoria, on the other hand, had no such feelings of secrecy regarding the body, but she did have an abhorrence of strong sunshine. Her skin was delicate and she was always under the impression that she would swoon in the heat, but never did. In 1858 she went so far as to give her husband, as a Christmas present, a life size statue of a male nude. Whether she had a true appreciation of its value as art or intended it as a broad hint, is hard to say. Deep down, she was somewhat of an exhibitionist. She would return from her bathroom clad only in a silk dressing gown which clung to the regal curves and left little to the imagination. Her grandchildren were somewhat shocked.

Yet it is obvious, from the discreet glimpses that we get in *Punch* of young ladies bathing, that the female form of distant yesterday was very different to that of to-day. The contours are reminiscent of the Chiltern Hills and certain it is that, if jeans had then been in fashion, Mama could not have borrowed Papa's. Those great, white marble thighs upon which the sun never shone have disappeared like the muffin-man and pumpkin pie.

These drawings of the seaside are among the happiest to appear in *Punch*. Crabs and sand, buckets and spades, sails and caves, ponies and donkeys, for the children, at least, the years between then and now have brought little change.

A SEA-SIDE DIALOGUE.

" Hollo, Jimmy !—Where are you a-going with yourn ?"
" Hesplanade !—Where be you ?"
" Prospec Place ?"   [*Exit Companions of the Bath.*

POLITE ATTENTION.

Lady. "OH NONSENSE, CHILD.—THERE MUST BE SOME MISTAKE!"
Boy. "NO, 'M. PLEASE, 'M, TWO YOUNG GENTS SAID IT LOOKED LIKE RAIN, AND I WAS TO FETCH YOU HOME IN THIS 'ERE CHEER!"

THE SWIMMERS.

Georgina. "NOW, CLARA, THAT'S NOT FAIR—YOU KNOW YOU HAVE ONE FOOT ON
THE GROUND."

"ALL VERY WELL."

Darling Nephew. "Oh, Aunty, come over here! Make Haste! Here's such a Beautiful Cave! Never mind your Bunions!"

AWFUL SCENE ON THE CHAIN PIER, BRIGHTON.

Nursemaid. "Lawk! There goes Charley, and he's took his Mar's parasol. What *will* Missus say?"

Bathing Woman. "Master Franky wouldn't cry! No! Not he!—He'll come to his Martha, and Bathe like a Man!"

DABBLING.

Master Jack (to very refined Governess, who has suddenly appeared). "Oh, Miss Finnikin, do come in; it's so awfully Jolly!"

A TYRANT.

Master Jacky (who pursues the fagging system even when home for the Holidays). "Oh, here you are! I've been looking for you Girls everywhere. Now, you just make haste home, and peel me a lot of Shrimps for my Lunch!"

WE SHOULD THINK SO.

Aunt. "NOW, CLARA, YOU SHOULD DO AS I DO. WHENEVER ANY MAN FOLLOWS ME, I TURN ROUND, AND GIVE HIM ONE OF *MY* LOOKS, AND HE IS OFF IMMEDIATELY."

SEA-SIDE CONFERENCE. SCENE—A WELL-KNOWN WATERING-PLACE.

Landlady. "*The price of these Rooms, Mum, is three pun ten a week, not one penny less. But stop, Mum, do I understand you to say that you will dine at home?*"

Lady. "*Yes, certainly; I shall dine at home, with the Children, every day.*"

Landlady. "*Oh, in that case, Mum, I can let you have the Rooms for two pun fifteen a week, and charge you nuffen for kitchen firing, Mum.*"

THE SEA-SIDE HAT—A HINT TO MATERFAMILIAS.

Harry (to Tom). "There's one great bore about a Watering-Place: they sell such horrid Cigars."

A JUDGE BY APPEARANCE.

Bathing Guide. "Bless 'is 'art! I know'd he'd take to it Kindly—by the werry looks on 'im!"

ADDING INSULT TO INJURY.

Nobbs, having come with his Family to the Seaside for a little Change of Scene, complains that they have been Terribly Bitten by—(But no, we will not mention the Horrid Creatures)—and is Addressed thus by the Lodging-House-Keeper: "Then hall I can say, Sir, his—That, if you've been hill-conwenienced by 'em, you must a' brought 'em down with you in your Portmantel!"

A DELICIOUS SAIL—OFF DOVER.

Old Lady. "GOODNESS GRACIOUS, MR. BOATMAN! WHAT'S THAT?"

Stolid Boatman. "THAT, MUM! NUTHUN, MUM. ONLY THE ARTILLERY A PRAC-*TI*-SIN', AND THAT'S ONE O' THE CANNON BALLS WHAT'S JUST STRUCK THE WATER!!"

TABLEAU REPRESENTING A YOUNG GENTLEMAN, WHO FANCIES HE IS ALONE BY THE "SAD SEA WAVES." HE TAKES THE
OPPORTUNITY OF GOING THROUGH THE LAST SCENE OF "LUCIA."

N.B. The Young Gentleman's voice (which HE imagines like MARIO'S) is of the most feeble and uncertain quality.

COMMON OBJECTS AT THE SEA-SIDE.

Boy. "OH! LOOK HERE, MA! I'VE CAUGHT A FISH JUST LIKE THOSE THINGAMIES IN MY
BED AT OUR LODGINGS!"

REAL ENJOYMENT.

Charley (who is wet through for the ninth time). "OH, MA! WE'VE BEEN *SO* JOLLY! WE'VE BEEN FILLING ONE ANOTHER'S HAIR WITH SAND, AND MAKING BOATS OF OUR BOOTS, AND HAVING SUCH FUN!"

A HORRID BOY.

Frank. "OH, I SAY, EMILY! AIN'T THE SEA-SIDE JOLLY?"

Emily (who is reading The Corsair to Kate). "I DO NOT KNOW, FRANK, WHAT YOU MEAN BY JOLLY.—IT IS VERY BEAUTIFUL!—IT IS VERY LOVELY!"

Frank. "HAH! AND DON'T IT MAKE YOU ALWAYS READY FOR YOUR GRUB, NEITHER?" [*Exit Young Ladies, very properly disgusted.*

AQUATICS.

Small Boy. "Now, then! All together!"

CROWDED STATE OF LODGING HOUSES.

Lodging-Housekeeper. "On'y this Room to Let, Mem. A Four-Post—a Tent—and a very comfortable double-bedded Chest of Drawers for the Young Gentlemen."

CAUTION TO YOUNG LADIES WHO RIDE IN CRINOLINE ON DONKEYS

NO DOUBT OF IT!

Invalid (in Carriage). "NOW, THESE POSTILIONS NEVER SEEM TO BE UNWELL! UPON MY WORD, I VERILY BELIEVE IF I WERE TO CHANGE PLACES WITH THAT LITTLE CHAP, I SHOULD BE EVER SO MUCH BETTER!"

Mamma. "NOW DO, GEORGE, COME OUT !"

THE STRIKE.

George. "I SHAN'T, IF YOU DON'T GIVE US BUNS AND MILK.'

Miss Stout. "THE WORST OF LETTING ONE'S BACK HAIR DOWN IS, THAT IT MAKES THE YOUNG MEN STARE SO!"

THE SEA-SIDE.—A CAPITAL OFFER.

"I SAY, GRANNY! CHARLEY SUMMERS AND I ARE GOING TO TAKE LION OUT IN A BOAT FOR A SWIM—NOW IF YOU'LL GIVE ME A SHILLING WE WILL TAKE YOU AND THE GIRLS FOR A ROW!"

A VERY GREAT MAN.

"NOW, COLLINS, YOU MUST GO OUT VERY DEEP, FOR I WANT TO TAKE A 'HEADER!'"

MAKING THE BEST OF IT.

A WATERING-PLACE YARN.

Youths. THEN I suppose when you were a smuggler you used to have reg'lar combats and fights?

Boatman. Com-bats and Fights! Lor love yer, we wos a'most always at it. Once in partickler I call to mind. There wos me and BILL BOKER (BLACK BILL we had used to call him) and four more had just run a cargo—(middle of the night it wos, and so uncommon dark you couldn't see an inch afore yer)—had just run a cargo of 'Ollands and pocket hand-kerchers—when we see about a hundred yards from where we wos—a comin' down the clift—the Coast Guard! Well! without saying a word, blowed if they didn't up pieces and let fly right at us. We fired agin—and—dear eyes! p'raps the bullets warn't flying about neither! It wos desprit wurk—we wos fightin 'most all night!

Youths. Lor! and which won?

Boatman. Oh—we won. But we was wounded awful! BILL BOKER was shot in the leg and in the barm—so wos JIM JAWLEY—and I had three balls through my head and two in the stummuck (wich I feel 'em now sometimes in the winter I do), besides bein' run through with a cutlass, and all my front teeth knocked out by the Perwentive man's telescope, wich luckily shut up or there's no knowin' wot might 'a bin the consequence. Ah! There *wos* goins on then. But lor, it aint nothin' like it now! [*Youths are deeply impressed.*

Chapter 7

TRULY RURAL

Punch was 'the London Charivari' and the countryside was a place apart. In the beginning of the period with which we are dealing journeys into 'the sticks' were slow and arduous, a matter of employing the few available trains as far as they went and then relying on the horse. By the end, the railways had penetrated most rural areas and a weekend in the country had become a practical proposition.

In the nineteenth century there were three types of village — the *open*, the *closed* and the *common*. The *closed* was lorded over by the squire. In the *open* the power was in the hands of the big farmers, and the local tradespeople and middle-class speculators who owned the property for profit. The *common* was a hangover from the period before land enclosure was applied in earnest in the reign of George III. Enclosure was still taking place in the mid-nineteenth century, 600,000 acres being fenced in between the Enclosure Act of 1845 and that of 1869. Then it came to an abrupt halt, when the British public realised that they were fast losing the right to roam as they pleased over areas which had been common land for centuries.

The population explosion of the eighteenth century had made enclosure a necessity. The mediaeval system of open-field cultivation, each man of the village having a number of unfenced strips, was both unproductive and uneconomic, and it was essential

105

that more corn should be produced. So the corn growing areas became a chess board of fenced fields. Nowadays, to suit the needs of the combine harvester, the fields are becoming bigger again, and hedges are disappearing.

"In the redivision of the open fields and common wastes among individual proprietors and farmers, there was no intention to defraud the small man, but no desire to give him more than his apparent legal claim. Often he could not prove a legal claim to the rights he exercised on the common. Oftener his legal rights to keep cows and geese there, or his personal right in one or two strips in the village field, were compensated with a sum of money which was not enough to enable him to set up as a capitalist farmer or pay for the hedging of the plot allotted to him; the compensation might, however, pay for a month's heavy drinking in the ale-house. And so he became a landless labourer."[1]

There were the people who clung to the villages which still retained a common, and common grazing. The men were rebels against the enclosure system. In the main they lived by grazing their cattle, geese and ponies on the common, but subsidised their income by poaching, smuggling, dealing and pilfering. Many emigrated, often under pressure from above. Strangers were seldom seen in the *common* villages, and certainly were not welcome, only those ready for a fight entered the public houses. If an artist had set up his easel on the common, he would have been treated as an enemy spy. The few 'high ups' seen in these parts were those riding to hounds, and the query, "Have you seen the hounds, my man?" met with a rude answer. In the drawings the boy sitting on the stile and the one leading a donkey are both children of the *common* village.

The *open* village was the most usual. Here the farmers held the reins of power, both for jobs and housing. Their sons went to the same school as those of the labourers, but there was a fence across the playground so that they could not mix. The class system was marked to the extent that, in a village with ten 'pubs', each man knew his own. Profit was a strong motive and there was little mercy for the unfortunate, the settlements for the lowly to be found at the end of green lanes in some areas being a positive disgrace. Yet in these villages there was a measure of independence and contentment.

It was scenes from the *closed* villages which appeared most frequently in *Punch*. These were on the estates where the squire ran everything. Sandringham in Norfolk the pride of the Prince of Wales, was one. Another was Helmingham in Suffolk, a haven of industry and peace directed by Lord Tollemache.[2] Here life was secure, neat houses and good gardens were provided, illness was cared for, hunger assuaged. There was only one snag — life in these oases demanded abnegation of self and ambition; to prosper, it was necessary to bend the knee. The freedom to think, act and behave as one would have liked to have done, had to be sacrificed; one became the squire's puppet.

The inhabitants had to agree to attend Church, touch their caps to Mi'lord and Mi'lady, clean their windows, dig their gardens with a spade and grow crops to an ordered rotation. Dress was regulated. The uniform laid down for farm labourers attending Church was corduroys, and Saturday nights had to be spent shining up their

[1] *History of England.* By G. M. Trevelyan. p. 611
[2] *Described by George Ewart Evans* in Tools of Their Trade

boots. Locals and the servants from the big house were not allowed to converse when assembling for the service; a Norfolk boy who had a word with a page was robbed of the restful interlude of Matins and was despatched to a nearby field to dig up docks. Girls were not allowed to smarten up their hats with feathers, and if one of them became pregnant before marriage, she was ordered to leave the village immediately. Her father, should he resist the order, lost both his job and his tenancy.

Game was the God on these big estates. Mighty battues, where half-tame pheasants and hares were shot by their thousand and the ladies joined their menfolk for lunch in a marquee, were the order of the day.

> "Game-preserving in the midst of a hungry population, with man-traps and spring guns lurking in the brambles to guard the pheasant at the expense of man's life or limb, led to a poaching war with armed skirmishes, and several thousand convictions a year. It was these contrasts that made the Radicalism of the new era, a spirit unknown in early Hanoverian England ...[1]"

Throughout the years since, the blame for this new Radicalism has been laid at the door of the old-English squire. In the event it was very little, if anything, to do with him. His hey-day ended with the coming of the railways and Queen Victoria; he was an isolationist, dreaming of Waterloo. Already becoming a rare bird in the 1860s, the death blow came in 'black '79' when the bottom fell out of the price of corn and the Squire had to sell his heritage for whatever price he could get. His sons were sent into the Church or the Indian Army or jobs overseas, and were warned that they must find their own security. The girls were told that their only salvation was to marry money, and not to worry about the class of its owner.

Mrs. Louise Cresswell, a tenant farmer at Sandringham when the estate was purchased by the Prince of Wales in 1862, wrote:

> "The Squire of the old school — is he disappearing from the scene to return no more? Shall we ever meet him again at the covert side, or see him shouldering his guns up and down the turnips — no new fangled ways of shooting for him — or riding round his estate on that perfect old grey cob, or laying down the law, spud in hand, to Giles the steward; in dress not half so swell as some of his own tenants, with provincialisms of speech contracted from addressing the said Giles and his subordinates in their native tongue ... untravelled and prejudiced beyond belief — what claim has he but a traditionary one to the social status of gentleman? Underneath that rough outside you find a kindliness and courtesy, a chivalry and honour 'sans peur et sans reproche', so true and just in all his dealings, scorning the sharp practice and lies of modern commerce ...."[2]

It was from 'modern commerce' that the new landlords came. Some had made their money from 'the spinning jenny', from coal and engineering, from railways and shipping. They had exploited cheap labour and children, and topped up their pile,

[1] *G.M. Trevelyan, p. 612.*
[2] *Whisper Louise* by David Duff. p. 64

107

with the easy profits which came as a result of the Crimean War. Some were brewers, for one could be genteel and brew, though not genteel and bake. Others followed Prince Albert, via the Great International Exhibition, from Germany and places east. It was these last who, with their highly developed capacity for making money, built the biggest new houses, laid out the most spectacular gardens and parks. It was this new type of squire who forbade the peasant his rabbit or hare and who sat in stern judgement on the Benches. Their star was Albert Edward, Prince of Wales, and they bowed to him and tickled his fancy as he danced, with tiring tread, on towards the bright light of kingship and the crown of an Empire upon which the sun never set. It was from these folk that sprang the Radicalism which showed itself in 1870, both in the Republican Movement and the Trade Unions.

As one follows *Punch* through the years, the change is clear to see. In the 1840s it concentrated on politics and finance, satire and hard-hitting. The mode of thinking and the reaction to events in the 1850s approached more nearly that of today than did the period which followed. Once the Prince of Wales had set going the gay music of his merry-go-rounds at Sandringham and Marlborough House, the rhythm changes. *Punch*

GROUNDLESS ALARM.

Equestrian. "Now, Boy, don't you be taking off your Hat to make me a Bow—you'll frighten my Horse."
Boy. "A—a—a warn't a-going too!"

was on the hall table of the rich new houses. People buy that which they like to read. In came the drawings of the battue and the hunting field, stalking in Scotland and first class trips up the Rhine, the Royal Academy and the *soiree,* Henley and the croquet lawn.

The golden memories of 'the good old days' come mostly from the *closed* villages, where those who sought the comfortable life fitted in with the squire's rules and did very nicely. The degree to which they were subjugated is, however, clear to see in the drawing of the little boy at the Church door, bowing to the two grand ladies who are followed by a page carrying a foot-warmer. That boy can only have been drawn from life.

Even if they did have to pick up stones on the way to school, and on the way back, the children of the country breathed fresh, pollution free air. They had the interest of the changing seasons, and fun and games in the leafy lanes. There was news value in the goings on up at the Hall, and there was the dream and the ambition that, one day, they would join the "carriage folk."

"Now then, Young Gen'l'man, we can't expect the Pony to drag us both up such a Hill as this, and as your Legs are younger than mine, you'd better get out and walk."

GORGEOUS SPECTACLE.

Sarah Jane. "Oh, Betsy, come 'ere, and bring Hisabeller! We can see the 'oofs of the 'Orses!!"

Boy. "*Oh, my! isn't that a beauty, neither?*"

Lady (who appropriates the speech to herself). "*Well, really, these country lads have more taste than the Londoners. I might have walked from Kensington to Whitechapel without having such a compliment paid me.*"

Gent on Horseback. "GET OUT OF THE WAY, BOY! GET OUT OF THE WAY!—MY HORSE DON'T LIKE DONKEYS!"

Boy. "DOAN'T HE?—THEN, WHY DOAN'T HE KICK THEE ORF?"

Polite Rustic. "OH! ARTER YEAOU, MUM."

FLUNKEIANA RUSTICA.

Mistress. "NOW, I DO HOPE, SAMUEL, YOU WILL MAKE YOURSELF TIDY, GET YOUR CLOTH
LAID IN TIME—AND TAKE GREAT PAINS WITH YOUR WAITING AT TABLE!"

Samuel (who has come recently out of a Strawyard). "YEZ, M'! BUT PLEAZ, M', BE OI TO
WEAR MY BREECHES?"

"I SAY, TOMMY, COME AND SHOVE. HERE'S THE POOR ORSES CAN'T
GET THE WAGGIN UP!"

EARLY PIETY.

Matilda Jane (catching the Pastor after Sunday School). "OH, SIR, PLEASE WHAT WOULD YOU CHARGE TO CHRISTEN MY DOLL?"

ART AT A CATTLE SHOW.

First Small Boy. "*I say, Bill, what's he a doing of?*"
Second Ditto. "*Can't you see he's a taking that old Gent's Picture, and* ISN'T *it like him?*"

OWING TO THE EXCEEDINGLY DRY WEATHER, MR. HACKLE FINDS THAT THE STREAM HE HAS
TAKEN FOR FISHING IS NOT IN SO GOOD A STATE AS HE COULD WISH.

Boy (attending). "No, Sir! nor there ain't bin none not for ever so long!"

LESSONS IN POLITICAL ECONOMY.

DIVISION OF LABOUR.

" Billy, you go and beat away the naughty Wasps, while I eat the Sugar."

Clerical Magnate, who has strayed a little from the right path. *"My dear child, can you inform me whether this is a public way?"*

Child. *"No, Sir; but come along o' me, and I'll show you the way to the Blue Lion."*

[His Reverence's horror may be more easily imagined than described.

A PROPER PRECAUTION.

Mistress. "THERE, SIR! THERE'S A BOTTLE OF EAU DE COLOGNE FOR YOU, AND DON'T LET ME HAVE OCCASION TO COMPLAIN AGAIN!"
Stirrups (the Party who looks after the Horse and Chaise). "YES, MUM! BUT BE OI TO DRINK IT?"
Mistress. "NO, SIR; YOU WILL HAVE TO WAIT AT TABLE TO-NIGHT, AND YOU ARE TO SPRINKLE IT OVER YOUR BEST LIVERY, THAT YOU MAY NOT BRING INTO THE HOUSE THAT DREADFUL EFFLUVIUM FROM THE STABLE THAT YOU HAVE HITHERTO DONE!"

A WHOLESOME CONCLUSION.

Lady Crinoline. "YES, LOVE—A VERY PRETTY CHURCH, BUT THE DOOR IS CERTAINLY VERY NARROW!"

Chapter 8

LES ENFANTS TERRIBLES

Here the 'horrible child' holds the stage — the holy terror whom one can only hope will be converted into a civilised human being with the passing of the years. Deep down, they have always been with us, but it seems strange that they managed to practise their wickednesses in days when a clout round the ear or a kick up the backside were the customary cures for precociousness. Perhaps, because there were fewer of them about then, they had bigger news value.

So, without further to-do, we sample their nastinesses — blackmail, rebellion, gluttony, snobbishness in age and class and gender, sneaking, dislike of water, and a touch of sadism. Some Mums never saw the warts on their treasures. Young Harry is a real 'stinker'. Let him kick the new maid if he wants to, says mother. It is just high spirits, 'the lion-hearted, sensitive little fellow'.

Inquiring Youth. "PLEASE, MAMMA, WHY IS UNCLE'S HORSE CALLED A *COB?*"
Mamma. "OH, MY DEAR! BECAUSE—BECAUSE—WHY BECAUSE HE HAS A THICK BODY AND SHORT LEGS!"
Inquiring Youth. "WHAT, LIKE YOU, MAMMA?"

A TERRIBLE THREAT.

Master Jack. "NOW THEN, CHARLOTTE, ARE YOU GOING TO LEND ME YOUR PAINT BOX?"
Charlotte. "NO, SIR. YOU KNOW WHAT A MESS YOU MADE OF IT LAST TIME!"
Master Jack. "VERY WELL. THEN I'LL PUT MY GUINEA PIG ON YOUR NECK!"

HOW VERY EMBARRASSING.

Gustavus. "MAMMA, DEAR! ARE MOUSTACHIOS FASHIONABLE?"
Mamma. "WELL, GUS, I DON'T KNOW EXACTLY, BUT I BELIEVE THEY ARE."
Gus. "OH! THEN, IS THAT THE REASON WHY MISS GRUMPH WEARS 'EM?"
[MISS GRUMPH, *as well as being strong-minded, is rather masculine in appearance.*

FRIGHTFUL CONSEQUENCE OF THE FROST.

Julia. "THE WATER WAS ALL FROZEN IN OUR JUGS LAST NIGHT."
Mamma. "AND SO IT WAS IN MINE, DEAR. WAS IT IN YOURS, CECIL?"
Cecil. "I DON'T KNOW!!"

DID YOU EVER!

Augustus. "I SAY, AUNT! DID YOU SEE WHAT THE NEWSPAPER SAYS ABOUT THE ECLIPSE?"

Aunt. "NO! WHAT DOES IT SAY? READ IT, CHILD! ANYTHING RELATING TO THAT WONDERFUL EVENT IS INTERESTING."

Augustus. "WHY, IT SAYS THAT IT IS EXPECTED TO HAVE AN EXTRAORDINARY EFFECT UPON THE INFERIOR ANIMALS! MY WIG! I'D HAVE YOU AND THE GIRLS LOOK OUT FOR SQUALLS!"   [*Disgusting, Low-Minded Boy.*

PRETTY INNOCENT!

Little Jessie. "MAMMA! WHY DO ALL THE TUNNELS SMELL SO STRONG OF BRANDY?"

[*The Lady in the middle never* was *fond of Children, and thinks she never met a Child she disliked more than this one.*

A SON AND HEIR.

Son and Heir. "How many of us are there? Why, if you Count the Girls, there are Six—but some people don't Count the Girls.—I'm One."

GRANDMAMMA IS SUPPOSED TO HAVE GIVEN MASTER TOM SOME PLUMS.

Master Tom. "Now, then, Granny, I've eaten the Plums, and if you don't give me Sixpence, I'll swallow the Stones!"

"So, Charley, I hear you have been to a Juvenile Party?"
Precocious Boy. "Well, I don't know what you call Juvenile. There was no one there under Five Years Old!"

Tiresome Child. "*I say, Aunt Gerty, when I'm as tall as Captain White, do you think I shall grow through my Hair, as he has?*"

AWKWARD PREDICAMENT.

Young Sparrow. "OH, I'M SORRY TO TROUBLE YOU, UNCLE—BUT COULD YOU LEND ME A RAZOR? MY CONFOUNDED FELLOW HASN'T PACKED UP MY DRESSING CASE!"

Aunt Isabel. "BEATRIX, WILL YOU HAVE SOME BREAD-AND-BUTTER?"
Beatrix. "NO!"
Aunt Isabel. "IS *THAT* THE WAY TO ANSWER? NO *WHAT?*"
Beatrix. "NO BREAD-AND-BUTTER!"

126

IRRESISTIBLE.

John Thomas. "Get away, Boy—Get away, Boy!"
Boy. "Shan't! and if yer don't let me Ride, I'll send this 'ere Mud over yer Calves!"

MISSUS-ISM,

OR WHAT WILL BECOME OF THE SERVANT GALS?

Proud Mother (to the new Maid). "*We parted with Sarah, because she was so sharp with our dear sweet little Harry, who has such animal spirits, you know; throwing everything about, or kicking his football through the window—perhaps he'll kick you, too—but you must not mind it, for he's a* Lion-hearted, sensitive little fellow!!"

Mrs. Smith. "Is Mrs. Brown in?"

Jane. "No, Mem, she's not at Home."

Little Girl. "Oh! what a Horrid Story, Jane! Mar's in the Kitchen, helping Cook!"

Uncle. "So, you've been to the Crystal Palace—Have you, Gus?"

Gus. "Yes, Uncle."

Uncle. "Well, now, I'll give you Sixpence if you will tell me what you admired most in that Temple of Industry?"

Gus. (unhesitatingly). "Veal and 'Am Pies, and the Ginger Beer. Give us the Sixpence!"

Chapter 9

THE COCKNEY KIDS

Punch's favourites among the younger generation were probably the poor children who roamed and played and worked in London's streets. They lived in slum dwellings and emerged to plague and enlighten the business and fashionable thoroughfares. The drawings are mostly of boys, for their sisters were held at home to help their mothers and care for even younger fry. They were varyingly described — street boys, street arabs, ragged urchins, juvenile vagrants. They came into the general category of 'the self-employed', for in truth, if they had not employed themselves, they would have gone more hungry than they already were. They were separate from the children who had regular employment, such as butchers' boys, office and errand boys, pages, 'tweenies', who were somewhat senior and find their place in later chapters.

These urchins swept street crossings and door-steps with tattered brushes. They blacked shoes. They were 'climbing boys' for the chimney-sweeps. They were link-boys, lighting the way, with their flaming torches, for those out late in the streets and the passengers from the railway stations. They held horses while the owners called at shops and houses. They ran messages. There were few jobs that they would not undertake for a penny.

They found much of their fun in repartee and making fun of people. Their victims were soldiers (volunteers in particular), fat old gentlemen incapable of fast pursuit, coachmen, old ladies attended by pages, young dandies, and, most of all, the footmen. It was the custom of these fancily dressed upper servants to pad out their be-stockinged calves with straw and other material, thus forming a target which no child, of any class, could resist. Prince Alfred, the Queen's second son, crept down the stairs of Buckingham Palace behind a footman and decorated his shapely calves with miniature flags of all nations, causing quite a stir at a regal function.

A FACT.

" Only a A-pen-y, Marm, just towards a new set o' Night Shirts, Marm."

By right and legislation, there should have been no 'climbing boys' for the artists to draw, but, in the event, it took more than a century to restrain the chimney-sweeps from using this method of carrying out their trade. It was in 1760 that the Quaker philanthropist, Joseph Hanway, took up their case with vigour and in 1785 he wrote a book entitled *A Sentimental History of Chimney-sweepers in London and Westminster, Showing the Necessity of Putting them under Regulation to Prevent the Grossest Inhumanity to the Climbing Boys, etc.* Hanway showed how illegitimate and orphan children were sold to the sweeps for as little as a pound each, which was less than the price of a terrier; how, naked and wild with terror, they were forced up the chimneys; how they were sent up to deal with chimneys which were on fire; how he had come across girls used for the purpose; and how the constant contact with soot brought on skin diseases, lung trouble and cancer.

Hanway managed to get an act passed forbidding the master-sweeps taking on children under the age of eight, but this regulation was so easy to get round that it had little good effect and for another half century the 'climbing boys' toiled and suffered, fell ill and died. It was not until 1834 that a determined effort was made to end the scandal. In that year sweeping machines were introduced and an Act was passed prohibiting the employment of apprentices under the age of ten, making it an offence to send a boy up a chimney to extinguish a fire and imposing penalties for ill-treatment. It was also laid down that, in the future, flues should not measure less than fourteen inches by nine inches, and that projecting angles should be rounded off.

Although the Act was good in theory, in practice it did not work. Sweeps would not put out money for machines, and in any case these would not clean rectangular flues, which were common everywhere. The builders, working at full pressure to cope with London's demand for more houses, had no intention of altering their plans to suit the convenience and welfare of small boys. It was left to that friend of children and the poor, Lord Ashley, soon to become Lord Shaftesbury, to come to the rescue, but even he only succeeded after a long and hard struggle. In 1840 he was instrumental in introducing legislation forbidding anyone under twenty-one from ascending or descending a chimney or employing an apprentice under sixteen. Heavier fines were introduced and further regulations made concerning the construction of flues. Still the master-sweeps and the builders snapped their fingers at the rules and, despite Shaftesbury's appeals to Parliament in the 1850s, it was not until 1864 that he succeeded in carrying a measure empowering magistrates to impose imprisonment with hard labour instead of a fine.

He thought that he had won, but still the grim stories reached him. In 1872 a 'climbing boy' was suffocated in a flue in Staffordshire. In 1873 one, only seven and a half years old, was killed in a chimney near Durham. In 1875 fourteen-year-old George Brewster was overcome by fumes, and died, at Cambridge. This was the case which roused public indignation at last, and the outcry was fanned by the newspapers. Brewster's master was sentenced to six months hard labour and Shaftesbury thundered: "One hundred and two years have elapsed since the good Joseph Hanway brought the brutal iniquity before the public, yet in many parts of England and Ireland it still prevails with the full knowledge and consent of thousands of all classes." With the wave of feeling to back him, in that Session of Parliament he succeeded in carrying a measure which finally put paid to what amounted to a national scandal, cruel beyond belief.

Thus it was, that throughout the period covered by this book, 'climbing boys' were still at their work. Certainly their lot in London was not so hard as in remote corners of Britain, unwatched by politicians, reformers and newspapermen, but they were considered a necessity in the task of maintaining older buildings. There is a story that one, lost and tired out, was found resting under the table in one of the Queen's rooms at Windsor. Here we see one, enriched with the French title of *ramoneur* and a donkey for transport, clearly still hot from a stint up a chimney, spending his hard earned penny on a strawberry ice. We see another, seemingly still in his single figure of years, requesting shelter from the rain under a fine lady's umbrella.

The message which flows from these drawings is of the courage of these street children and of their irrepressible sense of fun in the face of all adversities. And there was no fun for them except the fun they made. There were no sports for them, no toys, but 'crazes' were for free. Somersaulting was a craze for a time, and then standing on one's hands. If the well oiled gentleman going out to dinner did arrive with two bare footprints embossed in mud upon his smart new waistcoat, at least he would eat well and retire to a warm bed.

THE MAIN QUESTION.

Girl. "Any use of Me Waiting?"
Boy. "No; I only came Yesterday Morning, and ain't Half Full yet."

THOSE HORRID BOYS AGAIN!

Boy (to distinguished Volunteer). "Now, Capting! Clean yer Boots, and let yer 'ave a Shot at me for a Penny!"

"Oh! My!! Betsy!!! Whatever *his* the matter with your Doll?"

"Oh, he's always a ailin'; he's just had his Measles and now his face is took and broke out with the *mustarshers.*"

133

A CASE FOR LINDLEY MURRAY.

Cook (who is not in the best of Humours). *"Don't bother! No, I don't want none!"*
Boy. *"Well, leastways, you might ha' spoke Grammer!"*

MARLBOROUGH HOUSE ON A WET DAY.—(H.R.H. OUT OF LONDON.)

DOING A LITTLE BUSINESS.

Old Equestrian. " WELL BUT—YOU'RE NOT THE BOY I LEFT MY HORSE WITH!"
Boy. " NO, SIR, I JIST SPEKILATED, AND BOUGHT 'IM OF T'OTHER BOY FOR A HARPENNY?"

NOTHING LIKE BEING IN THE FASHION.

Exasperated Mother. " WOT ARE YER HAT—YER YOUNG HUSSY? AND
NOT A MINDIN THE CROSSIN, AS I TOLD YER."
Daughter. " HAT? WHY A DOIN SOME CROSHAY FRILLIN FOR MY
TROWSERS TO BE SURE. YOU WOULDN'T AVE ME DRESSED LIKE NO
ONE ELSE—WOULD YER?"

"BLACK YOUR SHOES, SIR?"

THE WEATHER AND THE PARKS.—GLORIOUS NEWS FOR THE BOYS!

Billy Wilkins. "HI! LOOK HERE! COME! SUCH A LARK! HERE'S A PERLICEMAN FELL ON A SLIDE!"

Officiousness of a horrid little Crossing-sweeper, soiling the Carpet with his nasty filthy Broom, and completely upsetting the Dignity of the whole thing

Boy. "PLEASE, SIR, TELL ME THE TIME?"
Crusty Old Gent. "YES, SIR,—BED-TIME!"

137

AN APRIL FOOL.

Equestrian. "HERE, BOY! COME AND HOLD MY HORSE."
Boy. "DOES HE KICK?"
Equestrian. "KICK! NO!"
Boy. "DOES HE BITE?"

Equestrian. "BITE! NO! CATCH HOLD OF HIM."
Boy. "DOES IT TAKE TWO TO HOLD HIM."
Equestrian. "NO."
Boy. "THEN HOLD HIM YOURSELF."
                    [Exit BOY, *performing "Pop goes the Weasel."*

Small Sweeper (to Crimean Hero). "Now, Captain, give us a copper, and I'll see yer safe over the Crossing!"

THE CROWDED STREETS.

Boy. "Now, Missus. There's no Busses, Kitch 'old of my Harm, and I'll take yer Over!"

First Boy. "*What does he do with all them Whiskers?*"
Second Boy. "*Why, when 'e's got enough of 'em, 'e cuts 'em off to stuff 'is Heasy Chair with?*"

Street Boy. "I SAY COOKY? THEY JUST ARE A FININ' OF 'EM ALL ROUND THE SKVARE—GIVE US A SHILLIN' AND I'LL SWEEP YOUR DOOR AFORE THE PLEECEMAN COMES."

Jacky. "HALLO, TOMMY! WHAT AVE YOU GOT THERE?"
Tommy. "HOYSTER."
Jacky. "OH! GIVE US A BIT."

A DREADFUL SHOCK TO THE NERVES.

"PLEASE M'EM, LET'S COME UNDER YOUR RUMBERELLER!"

A LUMPING PENN'ORTH.

"NOW, MY MAN, WHAT WOULD YOU SAY, IF I GAVE YOU A PENNY?"
"VY, THAT YOU VOS A JOLLY OLD BRICK!"

PROGRESS OF CIVILISATION.

Ramoneur (on Donkey). "Fitch us out another Pen'north o' Strawberry Ice, with a Dollop of Lemon Water in it."

ONE GOOD TURN DESERVES ANOTHER.

"Go it, Old Dusty, you're as good as a Fortun to us; so Tip us yer Foot, and I'll just give yer a Shine for Nothink."

THE FOG, JANUARY 21ST., 1865.

Link-boys (*Masters of the Situation*). "If yer don't give us a Shillin' we'll singe yer Whiskers!"

Little Boy. "Oh, my eye! There goes eightpence out of a shilling."

JUDICIOUS.

Little Boy. "STAND ON MY HEAD FOR A HA'PENNY, MARM?"
Old Lady. "NO, LITTLE BOY.—HERE IS A PENNY FOR KEEPING RIGHT END UPWARDS!"

Sharp (but vulgar) little Boy. "HALLO, MISSUS, WOT ARE THOSE?"
Old Woman. "TWOPENCE."
Boy. "WHAT A LIE! THEY 'RE APPLES."

[*Exit, whistling popular air.*

—AND, IT IS NOT A PLEASANT THING, WHEN GOING OUT TO DINNER, TO HAVE A SUMMERSAULT TURNED ON TO YOUR STOM— WE MEAN WAISTCOAT.

ALL FOOLS DAY.

Vagrant Juvenile. "HI! CAPTIN! YOU'VE DROPPED YER MOOS-TARCHURS."   [*Gent is arrested by a horrible feeling of doubt and dread.*
Vagrant Juvenile. "OH YOU APRIL FOOL!!"

" *Hooray! Hooray! 'Ere's a Johnny with his Calf falled down.*"

Ingenious Youth. "OH! SUCH A LARK, BILL! I'VE BIN AND FILLED AN OLD COVE'S LETTER-BOX WITH GOOSEBERRY SKINS AND HOYSTER SHELL,—AND RAPPED LIKE A POSTMAN!"
Old Cove. "HAVE YOU?"

145

DISAGREEABLE TRUTH.

Soldier. "Now, then! You must Move away from here."
Rude Boy. "Ah! But *you* mustn't, Old Feller!"

"A SELL."

Street Boy (who is no friend to Punch and Judy Shows). "*Oh, S' please S' ain't a Cove just a larruppin' his Wife up the Court neither!*"

146

CAUTION!

Prosperous Shoe Black. "*You don't ketch me putting my money into any o' them Banks, I can tell yer!*"

THE HEIGHT OF IMPUDENCE.

Blackguard Little Boy (to Queen's Coachman). "I SAY, COACHY, ARE YOU ENGAGED?"

A BAD TIME FOR JOHN THOMAS.

Rude Boy. "I SAY, JACK, AIN'T HE A FINE UN?—D'YE THINK HE'S REAL, OR ONLY STUFFED?"

THE ASCOT CUP DAY.

"WHY ARE YOU ON THE CROSSING, JAMES? IS YOUR FATHER HILL?
"NO. HE'S DROVE MOTHER DOWN TO HASCOT.

HOW DISAGREEABLE THE BOYS ARE.

Boy. "MY EYE, TOMMY! THERE'S THE HELEPHANT FROM THE S'LOGICAL
GARDINGS GOING A SKATING!"

" Ring vich! Vy, that von, in course.—T'other's only for the Flunkies."

Rude Boy. "Oh, look 'ere, Jim!—if 'ere aint a Lobster bin and out-growed his Cloak!"

POSITION IS EVERYTHING.

Betsy Jane (in confidence). "I shan't play no more with that Matilda Jenkins.—'Er doll ain't got no Perambylatur—and I don't mean mine to 'sociate with none but carridge cumpny!"

CAPITAL AND LABOUR.

Big Boy. "How do you make out Threepence is Threeha'pence a-piece? There's a Penny for my Broom and a Penny for my Shovel—that's Capital; and a Hapenny for you and a Hapenny for me—and that's Labour."

PAINFUL SITUATION OF A FATHER OF THE CHURCH.

" I say, Guv'nor, give us sixpennuth o' bronze for a Tizzy, to toss with Shiney Villiam."

A BRILLIANT IDEA.

Matilda. "OH, LOOKYE HERE, TOMMY! S'POSE WE PLAY AT YOUR BEIN' THE BIG FOOTMAN, AND ME AND LIZZERBUTH 'LL BE THE FINE LADIES IN THE CARRIDGE!"

REWARD OF MERIT.

Ragged Urchin. "Please give Dad a Short Pipe?"
...rman. "Can't do it. Don't know him."
Ragged Urchin. "Why, he gets Drunk here every Saturday Night."
...rman. "Oh! does he, my Little Dear? Then 'ere's a Nice Long 'un, with ... of Wax at the End."

"*Cattle Show, Sir? I'll take you all the way there for a Penny.*"

Sharp Shoeblack (loq.). "*Yes, Sir, I knows, Sir, Cooks IS wery pertic'lar.*"

151

A HINT TO THE ENTERPRISING.

Boy. "Here you are, Sir. Black yer Boots, and take yer Likeness for the small charge of Threepence!"

SEVERE.

Old Lady. "Ah thin, bad luck to ye, Grigory! where's yer Manners! One would think ye was in a Gintleman's House, standin before the fire with yer Coat-tails up, and Ladies present too!"

HEIGHT OF POLITENESS.

Lady. "*You deserve a Penny, my Boy; but I have no small change in my Porte-Monnaie.*"

Boy. "*Oh!* nang port, Mumselle, mercy tooley maim."

Chapter 10

IN THE STATELY HOMES

Here they are, the fortunate few among the young. Thoughts full of horses and hunting, parties and clothes, snobbery predominant. By the 1850s the wealth of the already rich was increasing so fast that the contrast between those at the top and those at the bottom was more obvious than of old. It was not that the poor were any less well off than they had been in the days of George III. It was the flaunting and the show of the new rich which stung and led to hate and envy. Thus it was that Radicalism flourished and showed its power in 1870.

> "The landed gentry . . . were enlarging the manor-house for the heir and the parsonage for the younger son, and too often replacing a tumble of gabled roofs that had grown up piece-meal in the last three hundred years, by a gorgeous 'gentleman's seat' in the neo-Palladian style."[1]

The Royal Family followed the 'big house' trend. First came Osborne, then Balmoral, then Sandringham. Prince Albert was for ever designing and building — ballrooms, stables, dairies, shooting lodges — and those who were new to the social scene followed wherever he led. Albert, like them, was also making money fast. His

[1] *History of England.* By G.M. Trevelyan p. 612.

allowance of £30,000 a year (which he considered much too small) was swelled by sinecures. He invested in property, art treasures and shares. By his acumen he increased the revenue of the Duchies of Cornwall and Lancaster from £32,000 to £126,000 per annum. He was a near penniless student when he came to England in 1841. When he died twenty years later it was estimated that he was worth half a million.

The old English families tried to keep up with the extravagance and lavish display of the new fast set which thrived on industry and smart investment. Some fell by the wayside, among them the Duke of Buckingham, whose creditors seized Stowe, when his debts totalled a million pounds. The Prince of Wales was 'in the red' by £20,000 a year as a result of the expense of keeping up Sandringham, but there was no shortage of volunteers ready to come to the aid of the Heir to the Throne. For many socially ambitious magnates, however, the stay in paradise was limited. There was the echo of clogs, and the clogs came back to clogs within a century, or even half.

The pictures seen here were drawn by John Leech. The detail of them is amazing, as if they were taken from a photograph. Everything is just as it should be on the breakfast table. No delicacies are missing at the children's party. The vicar is doing just the right thing at the village fete. Yet this tolerance of the rich was somewhat of an about-face for *Punch*. M.H. Spielman explained the change in *The History of "Punch"*:

> . . . As Mr. Punch went up in the social scale Leech accompanied him in the rise — if, indeed, it was not Leech, together with Thackeray's powerful help, who elevated *Punch* . . .

> "Mr. Leech," said Thackeray, "surveys society from the gentleman's point of view. In old days, when Mr. Jerrold lived and wrote for that famous periodical, he took the other side; he looked up at the rich and great with a fierce, a sarcastic aspect, and a threatening posture, and his outcry of challenge was: 'Ye rich and great, look out! We, the people, are as good as you. Have a care, ye priests, wallowing on a tithe pig and rolling in carriages and four; ye landlords, grinding the poor; ye vulgar fine ladies, bullying innocent governesses, and what not — we will expose your vulgarity; we will put down your oppression; we will vindicate the nobility of our common nature,' and so forth. A great deal was to be said on the Jerrold side, a great deal was said — perhaps, even a great deal too much." And now, says Thackeray in effect, Leech looks at all these people with a certain respect for their riches, with an amiable curiosity concerning their footmen's calves. Nevertheless to the end he was . . . not a whit more tolerant of viciousness, affectation, or meanness of any kind.

John Leech died in 1864, leaving behind him a pencilled tapestry of the life of his days. He caught the moment, left us a record. Swallow your negus boy . . . dance, dance, little lady . . . not for you to know that the poppies will bloom on Flanders field.

VERY KIND.

"WELL! GOOD BYE, UNCLE! I'VE ENJOYED MYSELF VERY MUCH IN THE COUNTRY; AND IF YOU WILL RUN UP TO LONDON AT
ANY TIME, I'LL SHOW YOU A LITTLE LIFE!"

"'TELL YOUR GOVERNOR THE YOUNG GENTLEMAN'S BELOW WHO WAS
IMPLORED TO RETURN TO THE BOSOM OF HIS FAMILY, AND EVERYTHING
SHOULD BE FORGIVEN.'"

"BEEN TO THE PLAY MUCH THESE HOLIDAYS, FRED?"
"AW—I WENT THE OTHER NIGHT. BUT, AW—I DON'T KNOW—SOMEHOW
PANTOMIMES ARE NOT WHAT THEY USED TO BE IN MY TIME; AND AS FOR THE
GURLS, THERE WASN'T A GOOD-LOOKING ONE IN THE HOUSE."

155

Master Sparrow. "LOOK THERE, TOM! YOUNG FRED IS ASLEEP!"

Master Sprat. "YES! POOR LITTLE BEGGAR! WHAT A SHAME IT IS TO KEEP SUCH A MERE CHILD AS THAT UP SO LATE!"

Cousin Florence. "WELL, TOMMY, AND SO YOU LIKE YOUR LITTLE FRIEND PHILIP, DO YOU; AND HOW OLD DO YOU THINK HE IS?"

Tommy. "WELL, I DON'T EXACTLY KNOW; BUT I SHOULD THINK HE WAS *RATHER* OLD, FOR HE *BLOWS HIS OWN NOSE!*"

Georgina. "WELL, GUS! AND HOW DID YOU LIKE YOUR PARTY LAST NIGHT?"
Gus. "OH, JOLLY!—I GOT ELEVEN ICES, AND NO END OF NEGUS, AND WENT DOWN FOUR TIMES TO SUPPER!!"

A WEIGHTY MATTER.

Frederic (a very big boy). "THAT'S A NICEISH PONY OF YOURS, CHARLEY.—BY THE BYE, HOW HEAVY ARE YOU?"
Charley. "WELL, WITHIN A POUND OF THREE STONE, I'M SORRY TO SAY."
Frederic. "OH! I CALL THAT A NICE WEIGHT. NOW, I'M OBLIGED TO HAVE VERY EXPENSIVE PONIES, FOR, WITH SADDLE AND DLE, I DON'T RIDE LESS THAN FOUR STONE TWO!"

157

BON-BONS FOR JUVENILE PARTIES.

Alfred. "I SAY, FRANK, ARN'T YOU GOING TO HAVE SOME SUPPER?"
Frank. "A—NOT AT PRESENT. I SHALL WAIT TILL THE WOMEN LEAVE THE ROOM."

ENTER MR. BOTTLES, THE BUTLER.

Master Fred. "THERE! THAT'S CAPITAL! STAND STILL, BOTTLES, AND I'LL SHOW YOU HOW THE CHINESE DO THE KNIFE TRICK AT THE PLAY." [BOTTLES *is much interested.*

How Young Gentlemen from school go to see a Pantomime now-a-days.

BON-BONS FROM JUVENILE PARTIES.

First Juvenile. "THAT'S A PRETTY GIRL TALKING TO YOUNG ALGERNON BINKS!"
Second Juvenile. "HM—TOL-LOL! YOU SHOULD HAVE SEEN HER SOME SEASONS AGO."

WAITING FOR THE CARRIAGE.

Charlie. "THIS WILL BE A STUPID AFFAIR, GEORGY."
Georgy. "OH! YES—ONLY A WHITE FROCK AND BLACK MITTEN PARTY—VERY SLOW!"
[*Old Nurse wonders what next.*

159

SCENE.—ROOM IN COUNTRY-HOUSE.—BREAKFAST-TIME.

Master Tom. "Oh, Robert!"

Robert. "Yes, Sir!"

Master Tom, "Oh, I say, Robert! The Ladies want me to take 'em out fishing to-day, so just tell Young Evans I shall want him to go with me to get some Wasp Grubs; and—Look here! Tell the Gardener he must get me some Large Lobworms directly, and a few small Frogs, as perhaps we shall Try for a Jack. And—Hi! Robert, tell him to send 'em in here, that I may see whether they're the right sort!

[*General exclamation of "Nasty Monkey!" from the Ladies. Old Gentleman, being rather deaf, wishes* MASTER TOM's *remarks repeated.*

CRUEL JOKE AT A FÊTE.

Horrid Boy (to his Cousin). "I say, Rose! Wasn't that Major De Vere who just left you?"

Rose. "Yes!"

Horrid Boy. "Ah, then, I think he might as well have told you what a tremendous Black Smudge you've got on your Nose!"   [*N.B. Of course there is no smudge; but there's no looking-glass within miles for poor Rose to satisfy herself.*

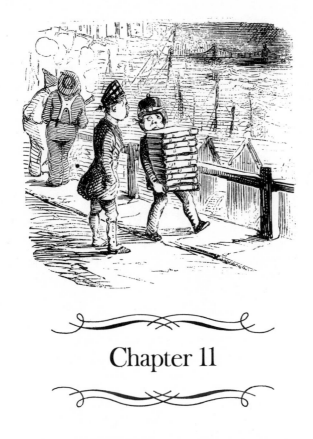

Chapter 11

POMPOUS PAGES

Boys who went into domestic service were given a wide variety of titles, although there was but slight variance in their tasks. There were boot-boys, knife-boys, foot-boys, coffee-boys, tea-boys, pipe-boys, 'backus-boys' and pages. Some boys were an admixture of them all, but the pages, with their old time definition of 'a boy attending upon a great person', regarded themselves as the senior. They wore buttons and in the 1850s and 1860s both boys and buttons were *de rigueur*. It was then considered vulgar to be waited upon at table by a woman and households of a certain standing included a man-servant or at least a page.

In the 1870s the parlour-maid came into fashion and pages began to disappear from private service, finding alternative employment in the clubs and hotels. However, specimens were still to be found at the beginning of the nineteenth century though and the Wodehouse era, one being put into secret training to run at long odds in the sports at the village fete.

A plurality of boys was to be found in only the stateliest of homes. There the boot-boy was kept busy in his den, polishing and boning the ceaseless supply of riding boots, shooting boots, walking shoes, evening shoes and slippers which appeared in the corridors. Guests might change their clothes three or four times a day, and there was more dust and mud around then. The knife-boy worked away at the steel cutlery, polishing and sharpening. If he was lucky, he had a machine into which grinding powder was poured and a handle turned the brushes. Tea-boys, coffee-boys and pipe-boys were apt to be an end-product of fashion and snobbishness. Princess Alice had a young Malay who travelled around with her and served the coffee. When she took him to Balmoral, his dark skin terrified the female servants, one of whom remarked that she would not like to do his washing as the black might come off. The Princess of Wales collected an Abyssinian donkey-boy while touring up the Nile and he was given the job of cleaning pipes at Sandringham and Marlborough House. Not having enough pipes to clean to keep him busy, he got into all sorts of pickles. He even ran up bills at London shops in the name of the Prince of Wales, which annoyed H.R.H. exceedingly as he was most careful with his own money. When all hope for the reformation of the boy had at last been given up, he was despatched to a clergyman for exorcism, and seen no more.

In the farmhouses of East Anglia there were holy terrors called 'backus-boys'. They spent most of the time on call in the 'back house' or scullery, and they pumped water, carried fuel, cleaned boots, held horses and ran errands. When important 'company' arrived, these none too sweet-smelling youths were arrayed in odd and individual uniforms and pressed into service as pages. The result was that the soup, should it arrive safely on the table, might have a subtle odour of horse manure.

The foot-boy was the embryo footman. While he retained the classification of 'boy', he was looked upon as an ally and playmate by the children of the house. When he was promoted to 'man', he joined the ranks of adult enemies.

By the 1850s the middle classes were imitating Queen Victoria. They continued to do so until the century's, and her, end. She had pages, albeit scions of the aristocracy, so the Mamas on the way up, and more especially their spinster sisters, must have pages too. These pages were largely for ostentation. They walked behind their mistress, carried her footwarmer and prayer books to Church, led her lap dog, kept an eye on her children, pushed her bathchair if she was immobile or lazy, and were at the receiving end of an unending diatribe of instruction and abuse. Because they were constantly on show in the streets, their mistresses made certain that they were smartly dressed and well fed. Thus the pages, unused to ample food in the homes from which they came, waxed fat.

We read of one in Thackeray.[1] Mrs. Captain Budge considered that her daughter should keep a man-servant. "It is proper, it is decent . . . In Captain Budge's lifetime we were never without our groom, and our tea-boy." There was a candidate available, one Grundsell who cleaned the knives, etc. He was elevated:

> His name was changed from Peter to Philip, as being more genteel: and a hat with a gold cord and a knob on the top like a gilt Brussels sprout, and a dark green suit with a bushel of buttons on the jacket, were purchased at an establishment in Holborn.

The bestowing of fancy names on pages was a practice much favoured. Here we see one named Adolphus, but the chances that he began life as the namesake of the old Duke of Cambridge are remote indeed.

[1] *Hobson's Choice, or The Tribulations of a Gentleman in Search of a Man-Servant.* By W.M. Thackeray.

RATHER HARD LINES.

"Now then! Adolphus!! Good gracious, what makes you stop so abruptly?"

"Please 'm, it's—"

"Oh! don't answer in that impertinent manner; but go on. (*Aside.*) He's evidently getting above his Work."

UNFEELING OBSERVATION.

SYMPTOMS OF WET WEATHER.

Vulgar Little Boy. "Oh, look here, Bill! Here's a poor boy bin and had the Hinfluenza, and now he's broke out all over, buttons and red stripes."

Tom. "Hollo, Sam, what the juice are you carring of?"

Sam. "'Clarrissa Arlo' for Missis."

THE ORIGINAL ROUND HAT.

Old Lady. (*loq.*) "WHAT CAN THEY SEE TO LAUGH AT; NASTY RUDE PEOPLE? IT'S A VERY SENSIBLE HAT—ESPECIALLY FOR THOSE WHO DON'T LIKE A STRONG LIGHT."

WHO WOULDN'T KEEP A FOOTMAN?

"LOOK HERE, JAMES!—OLD MISSUS IS GONE OUT OF TOWN, AND I'VE
GOT HER BEAST OF A DOG WOT'S FED UPON CHICKINGS TO TAKE CARE OF.
—WON'T I TEACH HIM TO SWIM, NEETHER?"

ACCOMMODATING!

STERN PARENT. "*Too Fat for a Page, you think, Sir? Um! You see, Sir, if so be you could wait a week or so, we could redooce him wery easy.*"

PRUDENCE.

Matilda (with the hat). "WELL, DEAR, NO ONE EVER PRESUMED TO ADDRESS *ME*; STILL, AFTER ALL THE LETTERS IN THE PAPERS, I THINK NO GIRL OF PREPOSSESSING APPEARANCE SHOULD EVER GO OUT UNPROTECTED; SO I ALWAYS TAKE THOMPSON NOW!"

THE MOUSTACHE MOVEMENT.

Foot Boy. "WELL, SIR, MASTER HIS AT 'OME, BUT HE'S CONFINED TO HIS ROOM. HE'S A GROWIN' OF HIS MOOSTARSHERS, AND AIN'T ALLOWED TO SEE NOBODY BUT HIS 'AIRDRESSER."

Page. "Fancy Ball, Sir? No, Sir! Missus's Fancy Ball, Sir, were last Toosday, Sir."

Boy. "Come in, Sir! You've no call to be afraid! I've got him quite tight."

A REVIEW AT CHATHAM.

First Boy. "BRING ANY O' YOUR 'OSSES DOWN?"
Second Boy. "No, I ONLY COME DOWN TO DRESS!"

" PLEASE 'M, HERE'S FIDO BEEN A ROLLIN' OF HIMSELF IN THE
' KETCH 'EM ALIVE, O!' "

CHURCH AND STATE.

A SCENE IN ST. JAMES'S PARK.

A GEOGRAPHICAL JOKE.

Impertinent Page (late from the dining-room). "I SAY, COOKEY AND SOOSAN, YOU MAKE A PRECIOUS FUSS ABOUT A FLEA,—HOW'D YER LIKE TO BE WHERE THE BLACK SEA SAILORS IS NOW?"

Susan. "WHERE'S THAT, IMPERANCE?"

Page. "WHY, MASTER SAYS IT'S WHERE THE BUG AND THE NIPPER (DNEIPER) MEET IN ONE BED!" [*Sensation and loud cries of "Oh!"*]

RUDE BOY!

Charley. "I SAY, ROBERT!"

Robert. "YES, SIR."

Charley. "I SUPPOSE YOU THINK YOU'RE A FOOTMAN, 'CAUSE PAPA'S GIVEN YOU A COAT; BUT YOU'RE ONLY A PAGE AFTER ALL, AND OUGHT TO HAVE LITTLE BUTTONS ALL THE WAY DOWN!"

Chapter 12

FASHION WISE

Basically, children are intrigued by change. It is as if they consider that the world, as they first remember it, is a constant; alteration to that way of life and looks becomes an object of curiosity and mirth. This applied more in the nineteenth century than it does today. Changes then were far less frequent. Today's children have hardly focussed their eyes on short skirts before long ones are in fashion — all most disturbing.

The Cockney kids of 1845 — 1865 certainly had plenty to laugh at, and plenty of cheeky remarks to make, in the field of ladies' fashion, due in the main to the ideas of Amelia Jenks Bloomer and Empress Eugenie of the French. To both these ladies, initiators respectively of the divided skirt and the crinoline, *Punch's* artists owed a debt of gratitude. Other fashions were to follow. George du Maurier thought that it would be pretty if every little lady wore black stockings — and so they did. Kate Greenaway dressed them up in smocks and poke-bonnets. Frances Hodgson Burnett set the fashion for black velvet Fauntleroy suits for boys. Children of all classes extracted most fun, however, from the crinoline. Here we see them using Mama's inflated behind as a carrying place for their prayer books on the way to church; converting the strange structure into a tent, Crimean style; extending little female bottoms by the use of mother's washing basket and watching, intrigued, to see how the grand, and very wide, lady managed to squeeze her diameter through a narrow carriage door.

As M.H. Spielman pointed out, there is value in *Punch* as a history of costume in the Victorian period. The artists put the spot-light on all the fads and fashions. In the masculine sphere, there were the gaily coloured shirts of 1845; the Joinville ties, with great fringed ends, of 1847; the cravats and cutaway coats of 1848; the ivory-handled canes of 1850; the bows and short sticks of 1852; the frockcoats of 1853; the schoolboy's Spanish hat of 1860, soon to be developed into the 'pork-pie' and worn with knickerbockers and the Dundreary whiskers of 1861, with which went a long coat, a long drawl and short wits.

Female fashions were even easier to follow. There was the coal-scuttle bonnet of 1845; bloomerism and cigarettes in 1851; bonnets worn off the head in 1853, and even more so next season. Crinolines came in at the time of the marriage of Eugenie to Napoleon, becoming bigger in 1860 and reaching their maximum dimensions in 1864. Eugenie also introduced the wide 'mushroom' hat — Florence Nightingale described her as 'the Empress who was born to be a dressmaker'. The 'spoon-shaped bonnet' was another little nonsense which came from Paris, the street-boys dubbing it 'the dustman's 'at'.

John Leech killed Bloomerism. He considered the American outfit both unfeminine and hideous, and he set about taking the micky out of those who indulged. In so doing he took a risk, for, bearing in mind the obstinacy of womankind, he might well have started a craze. As it was, with the disapproval of the age behind him, he won, and bloomers had to wait until the invention of the safety bicycle before they had their day. Even then it was said of them — "A skirt divided against itself cannot stand; it must sit upon a bicycle."

Queen Victoria was no fashion-plate, but she did much to popularise the parasol. Left to her own devices, she would probably have indulged more deeply in the creations of the Empress Eugenie, but there was a restraining hand on her shoulder. On one occasion her French *coiffeur* brought with him some of the latest fashions from Paris. He was showing them to the Queen when Albert walked in. His Germanic comment was brief. "That", he said, "you shall not wear."

A point which emerges from Leech's drawings is the importance that 'young gentlemen' attached to fashion. To those of very tender years, the change from a turndown collar to a stick-up and white choker was a step up the ladder towards the goal of mature man. A few years later they were prepared to 'give all their mind' to their hair style, their bow tie, the cut of their suits. Time is a merry-go-round and, when the repertoire is over, the same old tunes begin again.

Impudent Boy. "I SAY, BILL! COME AND SEE THE CONJURING—HERE'S THIS HERE GAL A GOIN' TO SQUEEGE HERSELF INTO THAT THERE BROOM!"

Young Lady. "*If you think you're a-going out with me that figgur, you're very much mistook. Where's your Gloves?*"

ECONOMY.

Mamma. "*My dear child! What are you doing with my best Velvet Dress?*"
Child. "*I am only cutting and contriving a Frock for my Doll!*"

175

HARRY TAKES HIS COUSINS TO SEE THE HOUNDS MEET.

Enter Mamma and Aunt Ellen.

Mamma (to Old Woman). "Pray, have you met Two Ladies and a Gentleman?"

Old Woman. "Well, I met Three People—But, la! there, I can't tell Ladies from Gentlemen now-a-days—when *I* was a Gal, &c. &c."

The Extremely Reprehensible Conduct of those two Podgkinsons, as they Walked to Church with their Papa, Mamma, and Sisters, the very first Sunday last Holidays.

"Please Marm, yer Bonnet's comin' off! Pitch us a Copper for telling yer."

Dreadful Boy. "My eye, Tommy, if I can't see the Old Gal's legs through the peep holes!"

UTILITY COMBINED WITH ELEGANCE.

IMITATION IS THE SINCEREST FLATTERY.

Sarah Jane to Betsy Ann. "Oh, yes! If it comes to that, you know People can stick out as much as other People—I always wears one o' Mother's Old Clothes Baskets."

"WHERE IGNORANCE IS BLISS."

THE TENT.

Podgers Quintus. *"Oh! here's a box o' Lucifers, let's make a fire inside."*

Podgers Secundus. *"Oh, come up-stairs, Katey, and play 'Soldiers in the Crimea' with us, and (sotto voce) we've got such a stunnin' Tent."*

Eldest Miss P. *"There, you may go and play with your brothers now, Katey, and don't get into Mischief."*

LA MODE.

Rude Boy. "OH, IF 'ERE AIN'T A GAL BEEN AND PUT ON A DUSTMAN'S 'AT!"

SOMETHING MORE APROPOS OF BLOOMERISM.

(BEHIND THE COUNTER THERE IS ONE OF THE "INFERIOR ANIMALS.")

SCENE.—DRAWING-ROOM.

Enter HORRID BOY.

Horrid Boy (*capering about*). "OH, LOOK HERE, CAPTAIN! I'VE FOUND OUT WHAT CLARA STUFFS HER HAIR OUT WITH. THEY'RE WHISKERS LIKE YOURS!" [*Sensation.*

LAYING THE DUST.

LADIES can, we know, sometimes go to very great lengths in dress; but the gown has lately got to such a pitch, and so much latitude is taken in the way of longitude, that there is no knowing where it will end. We have found, occasionally, very great inconvenience in our walks, by following, as excursionists, such a train as that which female fashion seems to entail on all its votaries. It says as little for the ankles as it does for the understandings of the fair sex of the present day, that they are compelled to hide their bad feet by at least one yard of superfluous drapery. In addition to the untidy and unsightly character of the proceeding, the dust raised is so great a nuisance, that every lady appearing in the costume of the period ought to be compelled to have a page in attendance, with a watering-pot, wherever she goes.

THOSE HORRID BOYS AGAIN.

Precise Female (in answer to a rude inquiry). "YOU ARE A VERY IMPERTINENT BOY!—YOU KNOW PERFECTLY WELL, THAT IT IS A MATTER OF NO MOMENT TO YOU WHO MY HATTER IS!"

IMPORTANT MATTER.

Augustus. "I SAY, LAURA, JUST TELL US BEFORE ANY ONE COMES, WHETHER MY BACK HAIR'S PARTED STRAIGHT!"

Enter Small Swell (who drawls as follows). "A—BWOWN, A—WANT SOME MORE COATS!"

Snip. "YES, SIR. THANK YOU, SIR. HOW MANY WOULD YOU PLEASE TO WANT?"

Small Swell. "A—LET ME SEE; A'LL HAVE EIGHT. A—NO, I'LL HAVE NINE; AND LOOK HERE! A—SHALL WANT SOME TROWSERS."

Snip. "YES, SIR. THANK YOU, SIR. HOW MANY WOULD YOU LIKE?"

Small Swell. "A—I DON'T KNOW EXACTLY. 'SPOSE WE SAY TWENTY-FOUR PAIRS; AND LOOK HERE! SHOW ME SOME PATTERNS THAT WON'T BE WORN BY ANY SNOBS!"

First Cock Sparrow. "WHAT A MIWACKULOUS TYE, FWANK. HOW THE DOOSE DO YOU MANAGE IT?"

Second Cock Sparrow. "YAS. I FANCY IT IS RATHER GRAND; BUT THEN, YOU SÉE, I GIVE THE WHOLE OF MY MIND TO IT!"

WE ALL HAVE OUR TROUBLES.

Sister Mary. "Why, Charley, dear Boy, what's the Matter? You seem quite Miserable!"

Charley. "Ah! aint I just! Here's Ma' says I must wear TURN-DOWN Collars till Christmas, and there's young Sidney Bowler (who's not Half so tall as I am) has had STICK-UPS and WHITE CHOKERS for ever so Long!"

Chapter 13

ACHES AND PAINS

The children of yesterday were seldom ill, and never for long. The usual childish complaints, such as constipation and feverish colds, or upsets caused by overeating or a surfeit of green apples, were dealt with by the administration of a dose or a powder, often most objectionable to take. Then, *ipso facto,* they were better. They had seen the doctor, taken their medicine — what else could a loving parent do? It was a convenient form of faith healing. If they contracted typhoid, cholera or pneumonia, they just died. God's will be done. Illness was not understood, and was looked upon as rather bad form and a bore. Families found satisfaction in singing that there was a home for little children above the bright blue sky and that little Arthur was playing with the angels by the stream in the Elysian fields — he was always so fond of paddling. In the event, in the nineteenth century the only excuse for not taking one's place at the dinner table was death. This applied right through the age scale and those who can remember the days of Queen Victoria will often show surprise at the number of people who are ill nowadays. It did not happen, they say, when they were young.

Yet in 1849 there were 16,000 deaths from cholera in London alone. One out of every two babies born in the towns died before the age of five[1], but it was not considered that they had been ill — they were victims of fate. This really meant that nothing

[1] *Victorian People and Ideas.* By Richard D. Altick. p.45

187

could be done about it. The Public Health Act of 1848 was a start towards eradicating the causes of these 'killers'; but it was yet too early, and it was not until 1872 that the Government put pressure on the local authorities to improve water supplies and sanitation. As Herbert Spencer said in 1852, it was simply a case of the "survival of the fittest"[1]. It was the work of men like Lister and Jenner, Simpson and Shaftesbury, and of a woman who was unique in the history of health, Florence Nightingale, which turned the tide.

Before their day faith played a large part in healing, and that faith centered on specialists in peculiar diseases. One woman in London society had three specialists, one for her nerves, one for her lungs and one for her heart. Similarly a farmer who was gored by a bull was taken by his wife to the cow doctress instead of the local doctor, as she said that the latter knew nothing about animals.

> "The idea is as old as the hills; a relic of the times when people prayed to St. Anthony for cure of erysipelas; to St. Martin for smallpox; to St. Vitus for nervous disorders; to St. Barbara for toothache, and accepted no cure unless they applied at the right shrine among the fourteen 'spiritual specialists'."[2]

It was not until 1830 that the principle was accepted that the general condition of a patient was more important than the local ailment, that disease was a change in him,

[1] Ibid. p. 232
[2] *The Life of a Century.* p. 252

THE THAW.

" Got the hinfluenza, have yer ? Ha ! you should wear
Hingyrubber goloshes as I does."

rather than in some part of him, and that treatment should concentrate on the whole rather than the local. The Encyclopaedia of Practical Medicine for 1833 recommended sixty drops of laudanum every two hours as a remedy for delirium tremens, but doctors often exceeded this dosage. If this treatment was not successful, the head was to be shaved and blistered. The cure for rickets, from which so many children suffered, was the application of leeches to the neck and forehead, coupled with repeated doses of antimony and calomel.

It was not only the poor who were denied the comfort of a bed during illness. Queen Victoria nearly died when she was a girl, the fever being variously attributed to typhoid or severe tonsillitis. Her mother would not admit that she was ill, insisting that it was her daughter's 'whim' to be so and that her governess was exaggerating. It was not until the Princess became delirious that a doctor was called.

In those days doctors believed in making certain that those who called upon their services *saw* that they were getting their money's worth. Belief and trust were not enough. The visual demonstration often took the form of quite unnecessary torture for the patient. George III, who suffered from porphyria, was terrified of his medical advisers, who would stuff him into a straight-waistcoat on the slightest excuse. When Queen Victoria's father, the Duke of Kent, was dying, the doctor decided that he must be 'cupped'. This entailed cutting into the Duke's flesh and covering the wound with a heated cup which, as it cooled, drew out the blood. The poor man was 'cupped' all over his body and even on his head. "For hours they must have tortured him", his wife later wrote, "and it made me nearly sick."[1]

Babies had to undergo their own peculiar torture when it came to vaccination. The first instance of this preventive step had taken place in the 1700s when Edward Jenner innoculated a boy with matter from the cow-pox vesicles on a milkmaid's hands. All the royal children were vaccinated, healthy babies who had already been so treated providing the necessary material. In the case of Princess Alice 'a magnificent baby' was produced and seated before her. "Such a duet of shrieks as the two kept up, staring terrified at each other, and ascribing the cuts, no doubt, to each other, instead of Mr. Brown."[2]

As for the young who wished to enter medicine, training began early. Under the apprenticeship system mere boys attended doctors in much the same way as other boys attended the plumbers. They passed such instruments as were required and filled the medicine bottles as instructed. By the bedside they listened to disquisitions on maladies of which even the names were unfamiliar and watched the examination of organs the operation of which they did not understand — a somewhat embarrassing ordeal for the patient. Here we see some examples, apprentices trying their hand at tooth extraction and dispensing. Apparently one role of the pupil was to scare away that bugbear of the doctor's life — the patient who did not pay. We see a very small boy with a very large knife, and the doctor tells his female victim that, if she does not get better, his pupil will put a 'seton' in the back of her neck. It seems doubtful, from the age and expression of the boy, if he had yet reached the stage of instruction when he had absorbed the knowledge that a seton was "a skein of cotton or silk, or a slip of india-rubber or gutta-percha, inserted in a wound to provoke and keep up an issue." On the other hand, it seems certain that the patient would not return to take part in such an experiment.

[1] *Queen Victoria.* Vol. I. By Cecil Woodham-Smith. p. 59

[2] *Correspondence of Sarah Spencer, Lady Lyttleton.* p. 339

Dr. Brown attended the Royal Family for many years.

Class was most important in the field of medicine. If a doctor was a gentleman by birth, he was accepted socially and landed the best patients. If a lady had to submit to having her intimate parts examined, at least let it be done by a gentleman. Few gentlemen followed the calling, however, and most doctors knew their place, they knocked on the side doors of the big houses and, if detained there, were content to eat alone. In turn, they were senior to apothecaries, described in contemporary dictionaries as "inferior practitioners."[1] We read in *Jane Eyre* of the apothecary being called in when the servants were ailing, while a physician attended to the family.

The Countess of Carlisle was on one occasion involved in a most difficult situation. She was taken ill and there was only a humble local apothecary available to attend her. She did not feel that she could discourse with the man directly, so a three cornered conversation took place, the Countess's maid retailing the messages, questions and answers between patient and practitioner. Eventually the apothecary informed the maid that it would be necessary to bleed the patient. The maid passed on the message and received the reply: "Inform the doctor that he *may* bleed the Countess of Carlisle."

[1] For a majority of country practitioners their status in 1840 was still merely that of a skilled tradesman, since their qualifying body, the Society of Apothecaries, was no university corporation but a Livery Company of the City of London. They were, moroeever, still not yet legally entitled to charge for advice without medicine, so as compulsory vendors of medicinal potions they could not be "real" professional men. Later, as the statuatory fee authorised was only 2s. 6d. per visit, they were still unable for financial reasons to hand over their retail dispensing trade to the chemists or druggists until the passing of the Medical Act of 1858. After this the Apothecaries left their shops and became "proper doctors", while the druggists, stifling their similar ambitions to pursue the road to medical practice, remained in theirs and became pharmaceutical chemists. As late as 1879, however, the metamorphosis was incomplete, for a correspondent complaiend in the Lancet that "some members of the profession still maintain shops in which tooth-brushes or hair-oil may be purchased!" Quoted from *The Apothecaries 1617-1967*, by Dr. W.S.C. Copeman. p. 55.

BON-BONS FROM JUVENILE PARTIES.

Doctor. "AHEM! "WELL! AND WHAT'S THE MATTER WITH MY YOUNG FRIEND, ADOLPHUS?"

Fond Mother. "WHY, HE IS NOT AT ALL THE THING, DOCTOR. HE WAS AT A JUVENILE PARTY, LAST NIGHT, WHERE THERE WAS A TWELFTH CAKE; AND IT PAINS ME TO SAY, THAT BESIDES EATING A GREAT DEAL TOO MUCH OF THE CAKE, HE WAS IMPRUDENT ENOUGH TO EAT A HARLEQUIN AND A MAN ON HORSEBACK, AND I AM SORRY TO ADD, A CUPID AND A BIRD CAGE FROM THE TOP OF IT!"

"WHY, WHAT'S THE MATTER WITH TOMMY?"

"BOO! HOO! I'VE CUT MY FINGER WITH AUNT'S SCISSORS."

"THAT'S A GOOD BOY! ALWAYS SPEAK THE TRUTH!"

A DOMESTIC EXTRAVAGANZA.

Mamma. "WHY, GOOD GRACIOUS, NURSE! WHAT'S THE MATTER WITH ADOLPHUS?
HE LOOKS VERY ODD!

Nurse. "AND WELL HE MAY, MUM! FOR HE THOUGHT THE COLOURED BALLS IN
MISS CHARLOTTE'S NEW GAME OF SOLITAIRE WAS BULL'S EYES, AND HE'S SWALLOWED
EVER SO MANY OF 'EM!"

YOUNG AND BRAVE, BUT MERCENARY.

DENTIST. "*Don't cry, my little friend. I didn't hurt your Sister very much—and
besides, your Mamma has just given her half-a-crown.*"
BOY. "*Boo-hoo! m-m-mayn't I have a tooth took out too?*"

DIFFERENCE OF OPINION.

Arabella. "NOW, CHARLEY, DEAR, *DO* HAVE A LITTLE COURAGE... WHEN *I* HAVE A POWDER TO TAKE, *I* DON'T LIKE IT ANY MORE THAN YOU DO .... BUT I MAKE UP MY MIND THAT I *WILL* TAKE IT, AND I *DO!*"

Charlie. "AND WHEN *I* HAVE A POWDER TO TAKE, I MAKE UP MY MIND THAT I WON'T TAKE IT, AND I *DON'T!!!*"

ADVICE GRATIS TO THE POOR.

Doctor. "YES, MRS. BROWN! YOU MUST GIVE HER PLENTY OF NICE PUDDINGS, SOME CALVES' FOOT JELLY—A LITTLE WINE—A FOWL OR TWO—TAKE HER TO THE SEA-SIDE, AND, IF POSSIBLE, GO WITH HER TO BADEN-BADEN."

"So you've taken all your stuff, and don't feel any better, eh? Well, then, we must alter the treatment. You must get your head shaved; and, if you will call here to-morrow about eleven, my pupil here will put a seton in the back of your neck."

MATERNAL SOLICITUDE.

"And the dear Children?"

"Why, Alexandrina Victoria is a good deal better; but dear little Albert here is still very delicate."

THAT HORRID MASTER BOB.

Doggy Young Gent. "*Ill is he? Hah! Sickening for the distemper, no doubt!*"

PUNCH'S CURIOSITIES OF MEDICAL EXPERIENCE.

Apprentice. "If you please, Sir, shall I fill up Mrs. Twaddle's Draughts with water?"

Practitioner. "Dear, dear me, Mr. Bumps, how often must I mention the subject? we never use water—*Aqua destillata*, if you please!"

DOCTOR. *"There's not much the matter with him, but I think we must cut off his animal aliment."*

MASTER TOM (with intense alarm). *" Oh ! Ma ! Will it hurt me ?"*

(AFTER A GREAT DEAL OF COAXING AND PERSUASION, MASTER TOM IS PREVAILED UPON TO PAY HIS QUARTERLY VISIT TO THE DENTIST. INCONSIDERATE AND VULGAR STREET BOYS UNFORTUNATELY PASS AT THE MOMENT HIS OBJECTIONS ARE OVERCOME).

First Inconsiderate Street Boy. "OH CRIKEY ! IF HERE AIN'T A CHAP GOIN' TO HAVE A GRINDER OUT. MY EYE, WHAT FANGS !"

Second Inconsiderate Do. do. "OH, I WOULDN'T BE 'IM. WON'T THERE BE A *SCR-E-W-A-U-N-CH* NEETHER ?" [*And, of course,* MASTER TOM *relapses into his previous very obstinate state.*

ALARMING SYMPTOMS AFTER EATING BOILED BEEF
AND GOOSEBERRY PIE.

Little Boy.—" OH, LOR, MAR, I FEEL JUST EXACTLY AS IF MY JACKET
WAS BUTTONED."

AN EXPERIMENT ON A VILE BODY.

Medical Pupil, after dragging a patient round the Surgery, succeeds in extracting a tooth. " COME !
THAT 'S NOT SO BAD FOR A FIRST ATTEMPT ! "

196

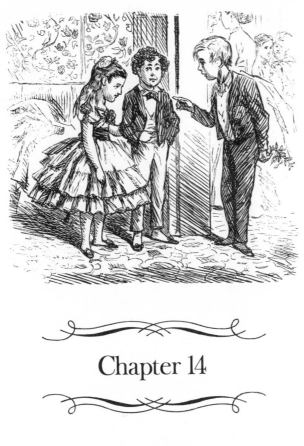

Chapter 14

LOVE

'What is this thing called love?' So ran the words of a song popular in the 1930s. As far as mid-nineteenth-century children were concerned, its interpretation seems to have been twofold, it was firstly, a stepping-stone towards maturity and, secondly, a means of blackmailing elder relations.

Kissing was apparently the 'in' thing; young gentlemen swopped osculation with the sisters of others in much the same way as they would peppermints or conkers, and they were not above sneaking on other indulgences to gain their end. There remains, however, the suspicion that, if it came to a hard choice, jelly took preference over lips.

There is a notable absence of romantic scenes between the children of the lower orders. That such feelings might exist at that end of the scale was not even acknowledged, let alone thought about. Certainly no encouragement should be given. As a young nobleman said after he had sampled sex for the first time, it was too good for the poor.

All the jokes about love were as pure as the driven snow. It was Thackeray's proud boast that *Punch* never published a remark or a drawing that could bring a blush to the maiden cheek. He thus addressed Mr. Punch:

"As for your morality, sir, it does not become me to compliment you on it before your venerable face; but permit me to say that there never was before published in this world so many volumes that contained so much cause for laughing, and so little for blushing; so many jokes, and so little harm. Why, sir, say even that your modesty, which astonishes me more and more every time I regard you, is calculated, and not a virtue naturally inherent in you, that very fact would argue for the high sense of the public morality among us. We will laugh in the company of our wives and children; we will tolerate no indecorum; we like that our matrons and girls should be pure."

Of course there were critics of this league of purity, there were hankerings after the sauciness of the Parisian magazines, and the suggestion was made that the editor should include such jokes as that about the girl looking at a monkey in a zoo and commenting, "He only wants a little money to be just like a man." Mr. Punch, however, was having none of that and adhered to his tenet that immorality did not exist.

One hesitates to contemplate what would have happened if any of the boys depicted in the following pictures had, in a moment of aberration and recalcitrance, given into the word 'Knickers'.

Mr. ——. "So, your Name is Charley, is it? Now, Charley doesn't know who I am?"
Sharp Little Boy. "Oh yes! but I do, though."
Mr. ——. "Well, who am I?"
Sharp Little Boy. "Why, you're the Gentleman who kissed Sister Sophy in the Library, on Twelfth Night, when you thought no one was there."

A CHRISTMAS SERMON.

(Dedicated to PUSEY, DENISON & CO.)

Lizzy. "OH, AMY, WHERE IS THE MISTLETOE?"
Amy. "THEY NEVER HAVE IT IN CHURCH, DEAR."
Lizzy. "OH, THEN WE MUST NOT LOVE EACH OTHER WHEN WE ARE IN CHURCH."

GROSS FLATTERY.

Emily. "GIVE ME A BIT OF ORANGE, CECIL!"
Cecil. "OH, AH! I DARE SAY! AFTER YOU'VE CALLED ME A PIG!"
Emily. "AH! BUT I MEANT A *PRETTY* PIG."

Whipper. "DOOCED NICE PLACE, THIS—ONLY ONE CAN'T SPEAK TO A GAL WITHOUT IT'S BEING REPORTED YOU'RE ENGAGED TO HER."
Snapper. "HAH! I TOOK THE PRECAUTION TO GIVE OUT WHEN I FIRST CAME THAT I WASN'T A MARRYIN' MAN!"

ELDER SISTER. "*Gus, there's your Cousin Rosa sitting down. Why don't you ask her to dance?*"
AUGUSTUS. "*Well, I've danced with her twice already, you know; and people are so disagreeable, if I trotted her out again, they'd be sure to talk about it!*"

A PEACE CONFERENCE.

Flora. "OH, I AM SO GLAD—DEAR HARRIET—THERE IS A CHANCE OF PEACE.— I AM MAKING THESE SLIPPERS AGAINST DEAR ALFRED COMES BACK!"

Cousin Tom. "HAH, WELL!—I AIN'T QUITE SO ANXIOUS ABOUT PEACE—FOR YOU SEE, SINCE THOSE SOLDIER CHAPS HAVE BEEN ABROAD, WE CIVILIANS HAVE HAD IT PRETTY MUCH OUR OWN WAY WITH THE GURLS!"

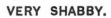

VERY SHABBY.

Rival. "THERE, IF YOU DON'T GIVE ME ONE, I'LL TELL YOUR BROTHER, 'CAUSE I SAW YOU KISS CHARLEY TURNER, JUST NOW, IN THE REFRESHMENT ROOM."

Juvenile. "OH! CHARLEY. IF YOU HEAR A REPORT THAT I'M GOING TO BE MARRIED TO THAT GIRL IN BLACK, YOU CAN CONTRADICT IT. THERE'S NOTHING IN IT."

YOUNG, BUT ARTFUL.

Frank. "I SAY, ARTHUR, I WISH YOU'D GO AND KISS MY SISTER! THERE SHE IS."
Arthur. "ALL RIGHT—WHAT FOR?"
Frank. "WHY, BECAUSE *THEN*, I COULD KISS *YOURS*."

203

Grandmama. "WHY, WHAT'S THE MATTER WITH MY PET?"

Child. "WHY, GRANDMA, AFTER GIVING THE SUBJECT EVERY CONSIDERATION, I HAVE COME TO THE CONCLUSION THAT—THE WORLD IS HOLLOW, AND MY DOLL IS STUFFED WITH SAWDUST, SO—I—SHOULD—LIKE—IF YOU PLEASE, TO BE A NUN?"

COMPARATIVE LOVE.

Papa. "SO, CHARLEY, YOU REALLY ARE IN LOVE WITH THE LITTLE BLACK-EYED GIRL YOU MET LAST NIGHT?"

Charley. "YES, PAPA, I LOVE HER DEARLY!"

Papa. "HOW MUCH DO YOU LOVE HER, CHARLEY? DO YOU LOVE HER AS MUCH AS PUDDING?"

Charley. "O YES, PAPA! AND A GREAT DEAL BETTER THAN PUDDING. BUT—(*pausing to reflect*)—I DO NOT LOVE HER—SO MUCH AS—JELLY!"

SHARP LITTLE BOY. "*Oh! I say, Pa! I know something,—I do.*"
PAPA (encouragingly). "*Well, Charley, what is it?*"
SHARP LITTLE BOY. "*Ah! I know why Cousin Tom and Sister Maria won't eat Onion Sauce! But I won't tell, 'cause Cousin Tom'll lick me!*"

THE DISAPPOINTED ONE.

Lover. "WHAT A BORE! JUST AS I WAS GOING TO POP THE QUESTION TO JENNY JONES,
HERE'S MY NURSE COME FOR ME!"

HOUSEMAIDS REFUSING SERVICE IN BELGRAVIA, (THE BARRACKS BEING REMOVED FROM KNIGHTSBRIDGE) YOUNG LADIES DO THE HOUSEWORK.

Lady Emily. "NOW, DEAR, I WISH YOU WOULD BE QUICK, AND LIGHT THE FIRES, AND HELP ME TO MAKE THE BEDS."

A VERY GREEN-EYED MONSTER!

First Juvenile. "I WONDER WHAT CAN MAKE HELEN HOLDFAST POLK WITH YOUNG ALBERT GRIG?"

Second Ditto. "DON'T YOU KNOW? WHY, TO MAKE ME JEALOUS! BUT SHE HAD BETTER NOT GO TOO FAR!"

Young Lady. "Now, then, you tiresome boy—What is it you wish to say to me that so nearly concerns your happiness?"

Juvenile. "Why, I love yer, and I can't be appy without yer."

SERVANTGALISM.

Mistress. "Not going to remain in a Situation any longer! Why you Foolish things, what *are* you going to do, then?"

Eliza. "Why, Ma'am, you see our *Fortune-Teller* say that two young Noblemen is a going to Marry us—so there's no call to remain in no Situations no more!"

Chapter 15

THE FIELD OF COMMERCE

You will find no upper-class money-makers in this chapter. In the mid-nineteenth century gentlemen did not enter business, and the very idea of their ladies doing so was *Punch's* idea of a very funny joke about what might happen in the far distant future. We get a glimpse of the middle-class attitude to commerce, but in the main the artists concentrated on the boys whose jobs entailed their appearance in the streets of London. Their sisters were tucked away in domestic service.

These boys worked for butchers, coal merchants, chemists, livery stables, offices and the railways. They were a cut above the street Arabs so beloved of *Punch,* for they had to have respectable homes and parental authority. They only received a few shillings a week, but at least that was regular. They are never seen in overcoats, even in the coldest weather, because they could not afford such luxuries. They worked from eight in the morning until eight at night, and there were no Saturday afternoons off and no Bank Holidays. For deliveries from shops, a pony was one step up the social ladder, and a cart the next.

Here we see the brighter side of their lives, amusement being the motive behind the pages upon which they appeared. Hidden away in the mean streets, in basements, sheds and attics, were working boys whose lot was not so congenial. They slaved in the grime and gloom of sweated labour. To them, the lot of the butcher's boy trotting his smart pony to the fine houses in the squares, was highly to be envied.

BAD HANGING. (DEDICATED TO THE R.A.'s)

FIGGINS, *our Coal Merchant, this Whitsun Holidays, has a Gorgeous Design painted on his Shutters (Landscape and Van); but see how the effect was marred by the injudicious Hanging of his Stupid Boy.*

A HORRIBLE BUSINESS.

Master Butcher. "Did you take Old Major Dumbledore's Ribs to No. 12?"
Boy. "Yes, Sir."
Master Butcher. "Then, cut Miss Wiggles's Shoulder and Neck, and hang Mr. Foodle's Legs till they're quite tender!"

Boy. "Mr. Pestle's out of Town, Mem. Can I give you any Adwice?"

Traveller. "NOW THEN, BOY, WHERE'S THE CLERK WHO GIVES THE TICKET."
Boy (after finishing an air he was whistling). "I'M THE CLERK."
Traveller. "WELL, SIR! AND WHAT TIME DOES THE TRAIN LEAVE FOR LONDON."
Boy. "OH, I DON'T KNOW. NO TIME IN PERTICKLER. SOMETIMES ONE TIME—AND SOMETIMES ANOTHER."

Purveyor of Poultry. "WHAT SORT O' PEOPLE ARE THEY AT NUMBER TWELVE, JACK?"
Purveyor of Meat. "OH! A RUBBISHIN' LOT. LEG O' MUTTON A' MONDAYS, AND 'ASH AN' COLD MEAT THE REST O' THE WEEK."

THE NEW GROOM.

Gentleman. "DO YOU MEAN TO SAY THAT YOU UNDERSTAND THE CARE OF HORSES?"
Boy. "WELL, SIR, I HAD OUGHT TO—FOR I'VE BEEN AMONGST 'EM ALL MY LIFE."

HORRIBLE SUSPICION IN HIGH LIFE.—SCENE, BELGRAVIA.

FIRST ARISTOCRATIC BUTCHER-BOY. *"Hullo, Bill! Don't mean to say Yer've come down to a Pony?"*
SECOND DITTO DITTO. *"Not dezactly! Our Cart is only gone a-paintin'."*

213

THE REMONSTRANCE.

London Merchant. "Why, what is the use of your being in a Respectable House of Business if you proceed in this absurd, vulgar manner? Now, take my word for it, unless you mend very considerably, you will go on from bad to worse. You will become a petty Huckster; from that you will, in all probability, get to be a mere Common Councilman; then an Alderman; when, after a course of Gluttony and Tom-Foolery, painful to think of, you will make a ridiculous termination to your Contemptible Career by actually becoming a Lord Mayor!"

THE EXCITEMENT IN BELGRAVIA.

Mr. Butcher *and* Master Butcher-Boy.

"Now, Bill, have you took the leg of Mutton to 29, and the Sweetbread to 24?"

"Yes, Master."

"Well, now your work is done—you'll take this bit of chalk and chalk up 'No Popry.' Do you ear?"

"Why, Master?"

"Why! Because 'Popes is enemies to butcher's meat on Fridays,' and Britons will have none of 'em." [*Exit* Bill.

Old Gentleman. "I WANT SOME SHAVING SOAP, MY GOOD LAD."
Boy. "YES, SIR. HERE'S A HARTICLE I CAN RECOMMEND, FOR I ALWAYS USE IT MYSELF!"

THE ALDERMAN'S ADVICE TO HIS SON.

Mr. Gobble. "YOU SEE, SAM, YOU ARE A WERRY YOUNG MAN; AND WHEN I AM TOOK AWAY, (WHICH, IN THE COMMON COURSE OF EWENTS, CAN'T BE WERRY LONG FUST), YOU WILL HAVE A GREAT DEAL OF PROPERTY. NOW, I'VE ONLY ONE PIECE OF ADWICE TO GIVE YOU. IT'S THIS—AND BY ALL MEANS ACT UPON IT:—LAY DOWN PLENTY OF PORT IN YOUR YOUTH, THAT YOU MAY HAVE A GOOD BOTTLE OF WINE IN YOUR OLD AGE."

Chapter 16

THE RISING GENERATION

We come, finally, to the stage when our children are growing up. It is time to say goodbye, for the young men are calling for their shaving water and buying their own cigars.

The Rising Generation was the title of a series of drawings made by John Leech in 1847 and a number of them are included in this chapter. They may be considered to be the origin of the expression used so often since — 'Goodness me! What are the young coming to? It would never have happened in my young day.'

The development of transport and communications, industry and science, was speeding up the rate of change in life and the young were impatient urging that the old order should yield place to the new. History repeats itself, and there is much to be found in common between the drawings of Leech and the young of the 1960s and 70s. There is the same rebellion against established custom and ideas, the same attempt to downgrade their elders, the same yearning for personal freedom.

It is apparent, however, that the change in outlook was reflected only in masculine circles. Except for a brief encounter with Bloomerism, when girls smoked and lounged about, the feminine element was subdued. In fact, we see a ghastly 'intellectual juvenile' giving his opinion, in a room full of ladies, that woman is an inferior animal.

In the 1860s there came an interesting switch in emphasis. The cheeky teenager disappears — no more drawings about teasing grandpapa or annoying passengers by smoking in railway carriages. The adolescent male had become a bore, nobody cared what he thought any more, and he was dismissed to the obscurity of school. His successor in the drawings was some ten years older, the man ripe for marriage. The pretty girl has the power now, even if she is playing second violin. Maybe the Crimean War had something to do with it: certainly the Volunteer Movement gave greater scope to the artist. Then there was the social revolution to be considered. The newly rich were installed in their new country mansions and were staging their weekend houseparties where romance was the order of the day and of the night. Hunting and punting, croquet and archery, dancing and the arts were in high fashion, and the poor old working classes scarcely got a look in.

There was another motive-power behind the change, none other than Albert Edward, Prince of Wales. Throughout his educational years he had been crammed and crushed, bullied and beaten, by his German father, Albert the Prince Consort. Here we see the famous cartoon of how Wales greeted his father on returning from his triumphant tour of Canada and America. In reality, it was not like that at all. Albert read his heir a lecture, stressing that the success of the tour was entirely due to his being his parents' son, and then despatched him to virtual imprisonment and hard labour at university. The natural result was that, when the Consort died in 1861, the Prince of Wales was soon out on the spree. 'Follow my leader', said the young rakes, and they hunted and shot, gambled and drank, smoked and flirted as much as they bally well wanted to. Children could not compete in news value, and so went upstairs with nanny and did jigsaw puzzles in the lamplight.

The twenty years through which we have passed were vital in the history of childhood. In them children became a talking point. We have been with them to the dentist and the tailor, we have been on holiday with them and seen them at their games, we have met them upstairs and downstairs, up to mischief in the mean streets and chatting in the country lanes. Maybe we have been sorry for the very poor and disapproving of very rich, but we must all have our favourites. For me, they are the Cockney kids, who, with much in their hearts and little in their stomachs, just kept marching on.

LATEST FROM AMERICA.

H.R.H. JUNIOR (TO H.R.H. SENIOR). "NOW, SIR-REE, IF YOU'LL LIQUOR UP AND SETTLE DOWN, I'LL TELL YOU ALL ABOUT MY TRAVELS."

First Elegant Creature. "A—Don't you Dance, Charles?"
Second ditto, ditto. "A—No—Not at Pwesent! I always let the Girls look, and long for me first!"

Gus (who is always so full of his nonsense). "Dash my Buttons, Ellen! that's a Stunning Waistcoat. I wish you'd Give us your Tailor's Address!"
Ellen. "Don't you be rude, Sir—and take your Arms off the Piano."

"THERE'S A 'AT, SIR! A STYLE ABOUT THAT 'AT, SIR!! JUST BECOMES
YOUR STYLE OF FACE, SIR!!!"

TO BE PITIED.

Youth. "WHAT! NO SMOKING CARRIAGE! WHY WHAT'S A FELLAH TO DO FOR THREE HOURS?"

Juvenile Oxford Man (who does not think Vin Ordinaire of himself.) "A—Were you at either University?"
Awful Swell. "Ya-as—when I was a—Boy!" [Oxford Man *departs in a Hansom.*

MISTAKEN IDENTITY.

Terrified Spinster. *" Oh, Mr. Policeman, I do believe here is one of those Ruffianly Libertines about to speak to me."*

GROSS INSULT.

UNIVERSITY *MAN* HAVING SPENT A FEW DAYS IN TOWN, AT THE END OF
TERM, IS ABOUT TO GO HOME.

Enter WAITER.

Waiter (condescendingly). "GOING HOME FOR THE HOLIDAYS, SIR?"
University MAN *(hurling himself into Hansom).* "EUSTON SQUA-A-A-RE!"

THE RISING GENERATION.

Old Lady. "NOW, ARTHUR, WHICH WILL YOU HAVE? SOME OF THIS NICE
*DDING, OR SOME JAM TART?"

Juvenile. "NO PASTRY, THANK-YE, AUNT. IT SPOILS ONE'S WINE SO. I
*T MIND A DEVILLED BISCUIT, THO', BY AND BY, WITH MY CLARET."
(Old Lady turns all manner of colours.)

First Juvenile. "HALF-A-DOZEN CHEROOTS, IF THEY ARE GOOD."
Second Juvenile. "AND I SAY, OLD BOY, WHILE YER HAND'S IN, JUST FILL
MY BOX WITH BROWN RAPPEE."

THE RISING GENERATION.

Hostess. "Now, my dear—Will you come and dance a quadrille?"

Juvenile. "Tha-a-nk you—It's so many years ago since I danced, that I would rather be excused, if you please. In fact, I,—aw, haven't danced since I was quite a boy."

THE RISING GENERATION.
"A HIGH-SPIRITED FELLOW."

Father. "In short, you are ruining yourself and everybody belonging to you by your extravagance and dissipation."

Juvenile. "Why, ya—as, there's a great deal of—aw—truth in what you say; but the fact is, my dear Sir, that I am, really—aw—such a creature of impulse—that—aw—that—aw—" (*Explanation dies away*).

THE RISING GENERATION.

Juvenile. "Uncle!"

Uncle. "Now then, what is it? This is the fourth time you've woke me up, Sir!"

Juvenile. "Oh! just put a few coals on the fire, and pass the wine, that's a good old Chap."

Youth. "HERE'S A NUISANCE, NOW! BLOWED IF I AIN'T LEFT MY CIGAR-CASE ON MY DRESSING-ROOM TABLE, AND THAT YOUNG BROTHER OF MINE WILL BE SMOKING ALL MY BEST REGALIAS!"

THE RISING GENERATION.

Juvenile. "WELL, I KNOW WHAT I SHALL DO: I SHALL LOOK OUT FOR SOME OLD GAL WITH PLENTY OF MONEY."

SOUND ADVICE.

Master Tom. "HAVE A WEED, GRAN'PA?"
Gran'pa. "A WHAT! SIR!"
Master Tom. "A WEED!—A CIGAR, YOU KNOW."
Gran'pa. "CERTAINLY NOT, SIR. I NEVER SMOKED IN MY LIFE."
Master Tom. "AH! THEN I WOULDN'T ADVISE YOU TO BEGIN."

Intellectual Juvenile. "Aw—WITH REGARD TO THAT PART OF THE—AW—AW—AWGU-MENT, I THINK—AW—THAT WOMAN IS DECIDEDLY—AW—AN INFERIAW—AW—ANIMAL."

ASTONISHING A YOUNG ONE.

Dick (to little Brother). "HAH! THIS IS ONE OF THE DISAGREEABLES IN BEING GROWN UP. WHY, BLESS YOU, IF I DIDN'T SHAVE TWICE A DAY THIS WARM WEATHER, I SHOULD NOT BE FIT TO BE SEEN!"

THE CORRECT THING FOR THE EXHIBITION.

First Little Gent. "DASH MY BUTTONS, 'ARRY! THAT'S A NEAT SHIRT."
Second Little Gent. "WELL, I RATHER LIKE IT MYSELF. IT'S QUITE MY OWN IDEA!"

GREAT BOON TO THE PUBLIC.

Incipient Swell (*in costume of the period*). "WELL! TA-TA, GUS! I SHALL JUST GO AND SHOW MYSELF IN THE PARK."

Stern Parient. "I TELL YOU, SIR, I WILL NOT ALLOW IT—AND DON'T LET ME SEE ANY MORE NASTY PIPES OR TOBACCO IN THIS HOUSE."
Young Williams. "BOO-HOO—AND WHAT'S A FELLOW TO DO WHEN ALL THE MEN OF HIS OWN AGE SMOKE."

227

CONSOLATION.

Young Snobley. "AH, JIM ! NOBLE BIRTH MUST BE A GREAT ADVANTAGE TO A COVE !"

Jim (one of Nature's nobility). "H'M ! P'RAPS !—BUT EGAD ! PERSONAL BEAUTY AIN'T A BAD SUBSTITUTE !"

Old Gentleman. "BLESS MY HEART ! THIS VIBRATION OF THE CARRIAGE IS VERY UNUSUAL ! PRAY, MY LITTLE MAN, HAVE YOU ANY APPREHENSION OF ACCIDENTS ON RAILWAYS ?"

Juvenile. "OH, NONE IN THE LEAST ; AND ESPECIALLY WITH SUCH A FAT OLD BUFFER AS YOU TO BE SHOT AGAINST."

Man of the World. "WHAT RUBBISH ALL THIS IS ABOUT MARRYING ON £ A-YEAR ! WHY, IT AIN'T ENOUGH TO BUY A FELLAH CIGARS !"